T0119757

Traditional Witchcraft and the Path to the Mysteries

Traditional Witchcraft and the Path to the Mysteries

Mélusine Draco

MOON
BOOKS

Winchester, UK
Washington, USA

First published by Moon Books, 2015
Moon Books is an imprint of John Hunt Publishing Ltd., Laurel House, Station Approach,
Alresford, Hants, SO24 9JH, UK
office1@jhpbooks.net
www.johnhuntpublishing.com
www.moon-books.net

For distributor details and how to order please visit the 'Ordering' section on our website.

Text copyright: Mélusine Draco 2014

ISBN: 978 1 78279 793 7

All rights reserved. Except for brief quotations in critical articles or reviews, no part of this
book may be reproduced in any manner without prior written permission from the publishers.

The rights of Mélusine Draco as author have been asserted in accordance with the Copyright,
Designs and Patents Act 1988.

A CIP catalogue record for this book is available from the British Library.

Design: Lee Nash

Printed and bound by CPI Group (UK) Ltd, Croydon, CR0 4YY, UK

We operate a distinctive and ethical publishing philosophy in all
areas of our business, from our global network of authors to
production and worldwide distribution.

CONTENTS

Dedicated to the memory
of
Mériém and Bob Clay-Egerton
who never swerved from the True Path

The Journey Begins ...
Kicking Over the Cauldron

A beautiful romantic dream of something that never was, never will be – in a light better than any light that ever shone – in a land no one can define or remember, only desire – and the forms are divinely beautiful...
Edward Burne-Jones

'Kicking Over The Cauldron' is not irreverence; it's an act of getting rid of the dross that often obscures genuine Old Craft teaching with modern-day propaganda. In *Traditional Witchcraft for Urban Living* we observed that an old-time witch might not have had the enquiring mind or educational opportunities of her 21st century counterparts, but she would have had the advantage of absorbing teaching passed on within an oral tradition that had persisted for hundreds of years.

The kernel of a traditional Old Craft witch's faith, however, is a belief in a definite association of force (or energy) within special localities, and the notion of natural universal energy influencing cause and effect. The term 'animism' was first coined in the early 18th century by Georg Ernst Stahl to describe his philosophy of a world soul; the word *anima*, meaning 'breath', which in Latin came to have the secondary sense of 'soul' = breath of life. The belief embraces the notion that spirits (or natural energy) inhabit everything in Nature – every hill, tree and stream, every breeze and cloud; every stone and pool has its own 'spirit' – although there are no authentic pagan 'scriptures' on which we can rely for guidance or comparison.

We should not, however, take this to mean that an Old Craft witch is spiritually backward, or lacking in tradition. The most amazing thing for us to consider, is that all this wondrous insight into the metaphysical and mystical world would have been passed down via an intuitive oral tradition, amongst people with no (or little) formal learning. In reality, it *is* possible to perceive ourselves as spiritual beings without being at all religious, because spirituality is how we 'feel' about the meaning of life – it is the quest for the hidden mysteries and need not necessarily manifest in religious terms. Lacking in intellect but not in application, the witch of yesteryear would probably have fully understood the sentiments expressed in a collection of spiritual essays dating from 1897, *The Treasure of the Humble*, wherein the author writes about *Ultima Thule* – the extreme limit – which also can be applied to the Mysteries of traditional British Old Craft today.

We are here on the borderland of human thought and far across the Arctic circle of the spirit. There is no ordinary cold, no ordinary dark there, and yet you shall find there naught but flames and light. But to those who arrive without having trained their minds to these new perceptions, the light and flames are as dark and cold as though they were painted. This means that the intelligence, the reason, will not suffice of themselves: **we must have faith**.

Nevertheless, in view of the historical backlash against witches, even in more modern times, it is not surprising that *'Trust None!'* remains the creed of traditional Old Craft and it has preserved its Mysteries by *not* divulging its rites and practices. No matter what a publisher's blurb may claim, there are no genuine traditional British Old Craft rituals, rites of passages, spells, charms or pathworkings in print, for one simple reason – any traditional witch committing any of this knowledge to paper for public scrutiny would be in breach of their own Initiatory Oaths. This still carries the ultimate penalty for treachery and betrayal. Admittedly, there are 'smokescreens' that may offer a *parody* of the genuine thing – but the gnarled roots of traditional Old Craft remain firmly in the shadows, where they belong. Although there may be a variation in formulae from region to region, the underlying Mysteries remain the same, and the only way to know about the Mysteries is to have experienced them first hand.

As always, when writing on this subject, I quote my old chum Alan Richardson, who wrote in his *Introduction to the Mystical Qabalah*:

> In magic there are the Lesser and Greater Mysteries. The former are the basic teachings whose intellectual content are available to all. The Greater Mysteries can only be understood through experience; they cannot be taught in words. The best that can be done is to provide symbols that the student may use as lenses to bring into focus his own blurred intimations of something greater in this world than himself. That is why it is useless searching books for any True Secret. It does not exist. Books and teachers can only give a few inadequate methods to reach the wisdom that is nowhere else but within the seeker.

It was also Andy Lloyd Book Reviews that first put the Traditional Witchcraft series into its proper perspective:

> The 'Traditional Witchcraft' series provides varied information about what it means to be a practising witch in modern times. In places, it feels like a guide, or self-help book. But there is much more to it than that. What strikes me is the amount of science running through the book. To understand nature is to live as a part of nature, and ultimately to become one with its changing patterns and cycles, to synchronise one's own psychic or magical energy with natural tidal forces and the elements. So a witch, like no other religious practitioner that I'm aware of, must study her environment carefully, and attune her life to it ... The learning

3

is multi-disciplinary, and feels almost as if one was studying a textbook written by a poet ... it has that sense of quiet wonder about it, supported by education, knowledge and, above all, wisdom.

In fact, the whole series was deliberately structured along the lines of a foundation course, so that any would-be traditional witch has a step-by-step guide to follow. *Traditional Witchcraft for Urban Living* (originally published as *Mean Streets Witchcraft*) was the first in the series and, as the title suggests, aimed at the majority of pagans who live in an urban environment rather than insisting that a witch must live in the country before they can learn about traditional Craft. The second step was revealed in *Traditional Witchcraft for the Seashore* that teaches us the importance of understanding and working with those natural tides within our own environment, even if we do not live by the sea. Step three, *Traditional Witchcraft for Fields and Hedgerows*, examines what most of us would think of in terms of traditional Craft, and brings us back into the comfort zone where we feel safe and secure – before step four casts us back out into the more hostile world of *Traditional Witchcraft for the Woods and Forests*: the magical energies differing quite considerably between these four environments.

The historical view of *Traditional Witchcraft and the Pagan Revival* was left until step five, because it's not until we've been studying traditional Old Craft for a while that we start to notice both the differences *and* the similarities between the various pagan disciplines. We *want* to know where our own beliefs come from; to trace these antecedents; and to understand why some of our ways are often diametrically opposed to those of other traditions we read about – and why. That is the reason for the fifth book in the series being written as a magical anthropology; simply to make sense of some of the things we've noticed but never fully understood.

Not that this method of teaching has always been favourably received. Some feel that Old Craft is portrayed as elitist, but as Daniel A Schulke observes in his introduction to this author's contribution to *Hands of Apostasy* ('Spirits and Deific Forms: Faith and Belief in British Old Craft'); 'All of these traditions share a common feature of extreme selectivity when it comes to prospective members, and the willingness to reject those proven unfit for the work.' Others claim there is nothing new contained within the books, or that there are no great revelations in the text, ignoring the fact that Old Craft learning is about 40 percent information and 60 percent intuition; but it's also about realising when intuition is telling us that we don't have all the information. There are books claiming to reveal the 'secrets' of traditional Craft – but intuition should tell us that if the secrets can be revealed in the reading of just one book, then the author cannot have that much to tell. The real secret is that *there are no secrets*, only a system of revelation that eventually leads to a series of enlightening experiences, and guides or teachers, to further our progress along the Path to the Mysteries.

Because of its occult (i.e. 'hidden') nature, traditional British Old Craft methods really do differ from region to region, so the opportunity of being in the company of genuine, traditional witches meant that late-night magical discussions were all part of the invaluable exchange of information that Old Crafters enjoy when meeting with those of their own kind and calibre. It was usually well past midnight when the cauldron would be kicked over; the dross discarded and the rare elixir of knowledge at the bottom shared and savoured.

Traditional Witchcraft and the Path to the Mysteries, the sixth and last in the series, is a voyage of discovery and, as with every journey, it is essential that we understand where we are now and where we want to be. We need proper direction unlike that popular old Irish saying: 'If I wanted to be going there, I wouldn't be starting from here!' So let us make our preparations, put our house in order, and begin our journey of exploration and self-discovery. As with all stages of life there are friends and acquaintances to consider: the essence of some we will take with us – the rest we will leave behind. But as the genii from *Where the Rainbow Ends* says: 'Time is short, and we have far to travel.'

Mélusine Draco: Glen of Aherlow 2013

Chapter One

Truth is Forty Shades of Grey (Sea)

Mystery: Phenomenon; circumstances or happening that cannot be explained; something obtuse or arcane; a truth divinely imparted; rites known only to the initiated; a sacrament.
[*Chambers Concise Dictionary*]

For the traditional British Old Craft witch the sea is one of the planet's great eternal Mysteries. Life on Earth started in the sea, while in esoteric terms it represents death and Otherworld. In this salt water environment we are reminded that the teeming marine communities of the ocean and coastal waters are powered by sunlight, by the nutrients dissolved in their waters, and by the forces that keep that water in motion – wind, the rotation of the Earth, and tidally induced currents. These forces are the oceanic currents that carry great masses of water round the world; one being that great 'river of the sea' – the Gulf Stream – which starts its journey in the warm waters off Mexico, and ensures that the climate off Britain is much milder than that of other places in the world on a similar latitude – i.e. countries bordering the Gulf of Alaska and the Bering Sea. Thereby demonstrating the force of the element of water within Elemental Water, to use a magical analogy.

The energy of the sea both destroys and builds. Coastal erosion is a scene of constant battle between the land and the sea and yet the sediments created by the outflows of the great inland rivers serve to create tidal mudflats that eventually reclaim the land from the ocean. From water vapour drawn up into the clouds from the deep ocean and falling as rain on the mountain slopes, the streams join the rivers to begin the journey back to the sea. In its upper reaches the river eats away at the land, but in its lower reaches it uses the material from the mountains to create new land at the seashore. Out in the deep ocean, water vapour is drawn up into the clouds ... as in magic there is the constant circular motion that echoes the saying: what goes around, comes around.

Witchcraft is not a religion yet it has a highly defined spiritual element to its practice. *Traditional Witchcraft for the Seashore* quoted the opening lines from Professor Barry Cunliffe's deceptively mystical book, *Facing the Ocean*, which begins with a highly evocative visualisation that encapsulates in a single paragraph how our distant ancestors looked upon the sea, how it shaped their lives – and the mystery that permeates Old Craft even today:

> To stand on a sea-washed promontory looking westwards at sunset over the Atlantic is to share a timeless human experience. We are in awe of the unchanging and unchangeable as all have been before us and all will be. Wonder is tempered with reassurance: it is an end, but we are content in the knowledge that the cycle will reproduce itself – the sun will reappear. The sea below creates different, more conflicting emotions. True, there is the comforting inevitability of the tides, but there is also an unpredictability of mood, the sea constantly changing, sometimes erupting in crescendos of brute force destroying and remoulding the land and claiming human life. The sea is a balancer of opposites. It gives and takes. It can destroy land and quickly build new; it sustains life and it can kill. Small wonder that through time communities have sought to explain these forces in terms of myth and have attempted to gain some puny influence over them through propitiation ...

These mystic elements reflect the 'Otherworldly' aspects of the sea, but as novelist Nelson Demille comments: 'There isn't a single mystery in this world that doesn't have a solution, if you live long enough to find it.' Here we return to the observation that Old Craft learning is about 40 percent information and 60 percent intuition, but most importantly realising when intuition is telling us that we don't have all the information. Needless to say, there is a lot of experience and know-how that lies in the back of what people call 'intuition', but age does have its benefits, and experience its inner knowledge.

From the esoteric perspective, the Mystery Path appears to have even more twists and turns, for although there are literally thousands of books on the subject of witchcraft, none offer up the secrets of the Mysteries, no matter what they claim. As Michael Howard reminded us in *Traditional Witchcraft and the Pagan Revival*: 'As [Robert] Cochrane said (and few people understand what he meant) witchcraft is not pagan, but it does preserve elements of the pagan Mysteries.' We are always conscious of this continuous cycle of destruction and re-creation, but at times it appears almost impossible to unravel the labyrinthine skein that leads to the heart of that which we seek. As *What You Call Time* explained at the beginning:

> Anyone seriously exploring the realms of occultism will soon discover they are hard pressed to find a comprehensive textbook on the subject ... Like smoke from the Abyss, curling tendrils of misinformation cloud the issue until the seeker chokes of the sulphurous fumes of their own research. Infernal demons hound and harry the unwary along a series of blind alleyways with conflicting directions and deliberately misleading instructions. Following the darkened maze, through endless sloping corridors to a distorted hall of mirrors, the seeker emerges into the light no wiser than when they began their quest.

We can also find that the old adage to be 'all at sea' i.e., wide of the mark, quite wrong – like a person in the open sea without a compass or chart – is often the position in which many witches find themselves when trying to discover the beginning of the Path to the Mysteries. Not only do they encounter confusion, but often also isolation because the very people with whom they've worked and trusted have turned their backs and walked away without explanation. Neither is it unusual to be asked to leave a coven or group following a request for further instruction on a deeper level. Those with genuine ability can also fall foul of other members with lesser ability but who wish to curry favour with the leader who, in turn, may feel undermined by such requests. Jealousy, spite and 'bad-mouthing' are prevalent in most elements of paganism, but it often means that the genuine seeker can spend the next ten years in 'the wilderness' because of what may be viewed as the short sightedness of others.

In reality, this is a natural progression within Old Craft, just as it is natural for animals in the wild to turn out this year's young to fend for themselves once they reach maturity. There seems to be some internal safety mechanism that dictates promising 'seekers' should be cut loose before they become too complacent and safe within the comfy zone of the group. The Path to the Mysteries is long and hazardous, and often the group leader will wisely accept that they do not have the experience to guide that particular seeker any further and must therefore let them go. Even if they are excellent tutors, there may be a question of avoiding cutting a favourite student too much slack in allowing things to go unchecked that should be corrected, thereby hampering their ultimate Initiation into the Mysteries. It is often following these 'wilderness' years, however, that another esoteric saying comes into play: 'When the student is ready, the teacher appears.'

At this point we also need to go into the uncharted waters of 'Initiation' in order to clarify what is meant by this in traditional British Old Craft. Initiation is a word rich in symbolism and meaning, and because it is a term that describes a *personal* experience, it goes without saying that the experience can be viewed on many different levels. When used in a modern sense, it is nearly always associated with the preparation for, and undergoing, a group participation initiatory ceremony or ritual as acceptance into that particular group or Tradition. For a traditional witch undergoing Initiation into the Mystery Tradition, it is a word associated with a solitary, life-changing (and often life-threatening) experience. It represents a true test that cannot be revised for – or cheated at – and is something that requires proper explanation and a considerable amount of correct preparation, by both student *and* teacher.

Within the magical or pagan community (and I use the terms very generally) the word 'Initiation' has been bandied about until it has become somewhat profaned. As Aleister Crowley points out, in ancient times, 'a young man would go into the Temple to be initiated and he would know perfectly well that his life might depend on his proving himself worthy. Nowadays the candidate knows that his initiators will not murder him, and any ordeal proposed by them obviously appears a pure formality.' Among many self-taught pagans 'Initiation' is often used to describe something that a true Initiate would refer to as a 'rite of dedication'. And while a rite of dedication can be a very important and deeply moving experience, it should not be confused, or equated with, true Initiation into the Mysteries.

Initiation in the esoteric sense means recognition that a witch has reached a required level of Understanding, which indicates that they are ready to submit themselves to being seriously tested on the physical, magical and spiritual levels. In the good old days, however, it was often said that anyone undergoing *mystical* Initiation came through enlightened, insane or dead! And, to a certain extent, this remains a truism with some Old Craft contemporary rites – even today. So, while the outward emphasis may still be on the Initiate, the responsibilities for encouraging someone to undergo an important rite such as this, actually lies heavily on the shoulders of the teacher, or Elders, of the coven or order (together with the guidance of the 'deities' involved).

For those belonging to traditional British Old Craft, the general feeling in recent years concerning the modern trend for acquiring degrees, ranks and titles as fast as possible is that this has led to an overall lowering of standards. This compromising of the Old Ways now has resulted in self-styled 'weekend course gurus', who are far more interested in acquiring a dubious kind of kudos, offering instruction to totally unsuitable and ill-prepared people. This form of numbers game means the kudos is gained merely on the basis of having initiated X number of people regardless of whether the rites were either appropriate or successful. It should be glaringly obvious that in the long run these people are doing more harm than good, not only to the innocent students involved, but also to the meaning of the actual Mysteries themselves.

The aim of those still following the Old Ways within authentic traditional groups is to re-establish the true meaning of Initiation. By maintaining the necessary dedication and a true spirit of respect for what mystical training should be, they pride themselves on continuing to perpetuate the old-fashioned high standards when it comes to teaching and Initiation. Those decisions are not merely based on an individual student's intellect, but also on an understanding of what *really* lies behind their interest in mysticism. Initiation into the Old Craft Mysteries is dangerous and littered with pitfalls, and that is why Old Craft teachers take the responsibility of ensuring the would-be Initiate doesn't go mad or drop dead during the rite! We know from first-hand experience within our own Tradition, of those who have 'lost it' during the procedure, and so take every possible precaution to guide and protect prior to, during, and for some time after the event.

Few also realise the amount of dedication and sheer hard

work that goes into a formal Initiation from the position of the teachers themselves. Firstly, there are the years of personal study and experimentation; the blood, sweat and tears that have been poured into the gaining of knowledge, wisdom and under-standing of the Universal Mysteries. Contrary to popular belief, this is an ongoing thing, since no one but a fool would ever reach a point of thinking: *'That's it! I cannot learn any more'*. As well as teaching, teachers are continuing to learn and always adding to their own store of that precious Knowledge, Wisdom and Understanding.

Secondly, there is a long period of preparation – often over many years – in readiness for shouldering the responsibility of guiding others along the path. This is a complex and often overlooked area, but a good teacher has to know that they are capable of dealing with any situation as it may arise, and dealing with it correctly on a personal, magical, mystical and practical level. Teachers also have to be capable of making difficult choices, and in some cases, even refusing instruction for Initiation, based on sound reasoning and magical laws. Needless to say, tact and diplomacy, coupled with magical abilities are prerequisites in such cases, *especially* when duty forces us to over-ride personal friendships.

Why Should we Bother with the Mysteries?

Whether we like the idea or not, our dead are always with us ... but this does not mean we are perpetually haunted by the shades of deceased, wrinkly and cantankerous relatives. Neither does it mean that the newly deceased will be kept earth-bound, in a state of limbo, in case they are needed on matters of earthly importance by those left behind. Our 'Ancestors' represent our culture, traditions, heritage, lineage and antecedents; they trace the long, tortuous march of history that our predecessors have taken under the aegis of traditional British Old Craft.

When those of a particular Tradition pass beyond the veil,

their spiritual essence merges with the divine spirit of the Whole, which in turn gives traditional British Old Craft the continuing power to endure – even past its own time and place in history. It therefore remains the duty of an Old Craft witch to ensure that the soul of any newly deceased can successfully join the Ancestors and keep adding to the strength of belief, which, in many instances may already have endured for hundreds of years. This is why it is so important for the proper funerary rites to be conducted by a genuine Initiate of the appropriate Mysteries. If when living, we cannot acknowledge and respect the Ancestors of traditional British Old Craft to which we *claim* to belong, then we will contribute nothing to the Whole when we die.

The honouring of the dead and venerating their memory is a common root of all religion, with many cultures believing that the dead live on in another dimension, continuing to affect the lives of subsequent generations. This concept of spirit-Ancestors is an extremely ancient one, especially when it involves dealing with deceased members of a particular people or clan, and is still widely observed in Japanese Shinto, Chinese Confucianism and among the Australian aboriginal and Amerindian peoples. In the West, we know from the prehistoric remains of the numerous earthworks that the indigenous people of the British Isles and the incoming Celts honoured their ancestors; and the earliest written observations are those of the Roman *Paternalia* (February) and the *Lemuria* (May), which later spread throughout the Empire.

Interaction with these spirit-Ancestors as an invisible and powerful presence is a constant feature of traditional British Old Craft, with the Ancestors remaining important members of the Tradition and people they have left behind. In general they are seen as Elders, treated and referred to in much the same way as the most senior of living Elders of a coven or magical group, with additional mystical and/or magical powers. Sometimes they are identified as the Holy Guardian Angel, the Mighty Dead, the Watchers, or the Old Ones, who gave magical knowledge to mankind, rather than merely family or tribal dead. Or, even more ambiguously 'those who have gone before' – their magical essence distilled into the universal subconscious at different levels.

Reverence for Old Craft Ancestors is part of the ethic of respect for those who have preceded us in life, and their continued presence on the periphery of our consciousness means that they are always with us. And because traditional witchcraft is essentially a practical thing, the Ancestors are called upon to help find solutions to magical problems through divination, pathworking and spellcasting. Although witchcraft is *not* a religion, the belief in the ancestral spirits goes hand in hand with a deep reverence for Nature and the 'spirits' that inhabit the landscape.

Once contact has been established, the Ancestors can be relied upon to have the interests of the 'tradition' – and therefore the individual witch's interests – as their primary concern. This belief reflects the profound importance of kinship in the ordering of Old Craft society. The Ancestors protect the living, but insist on the maintenance of various customs, and any serious breach of etiquette could result in the removal of their favour.

All Hallows or Samhain is the beginning of the dark, winter half of the year and a time for honouring the Ancestors, which is a sombre occasion in the witch's year and certainly not a time for celebration. To use a familiar phrase, 'it is when the veil between the worlds is at its thinnest', and a candle placed at the window can call the Ancestors home. Some traditional witches hold a Dumb Supper to mark the occasion, setting an empty place at the table for any wandering ancestral spirit who cares to partake of the offerings.

> ... *And heavy is the tread*
> *Of the living; but the dead*
> *Returning lightly dance ...*

From pre-Christian times, this darkening time of the year has been associated with ancestral spirits, unquiet ghosts and death. Ritual fires were kindled on hilltops for the purification of the people and the land, but unlike the Bel-fires that were lit at dawn, the Hallow-fires were lit at dusk. Much of what we see in the towns that pass for Hallowe'en rites are imported from America, although this is *not* a time for trick and treating! The festival should be observed as a means of demonstrating Craft unity to outsiders, while at the same time ritually remembering the Ancestors and reinforcing the heritage of traditional witchcraft. These observations and subsequent teaching of traditional Ancestor worship within the practice of witchcraft plays an important role in ensuring the continuity of the Tradition.

So we are back where we started – acknowledging that the sea is one of the Planet's eternal Mysteries; that the continuous cycle of life-death-rebirth starts and ends in the sea; and that in esoteric terms the sea signifies death and Otherworld, i.e. the realm of the Ancestors. Nevertheless, Maurice Maeterlinck managed to write in *Death,* an extremely concise view of immortality, which reflects the metaphysical stance of many of the Mysteries, especially for those with a grasp of Qabalistic philosophy:

Total annihilation is impossible. We are prisoners of an infinity without outlet, wherein nothing perishes, wherein everything is dispersed, but nothing lost. Neither a body nor a thought can drop out of the universe, out of time and space. Not an atom of our flesh, nor a quiver of our nerves, will go where they will cease to be, for there is no place where anything ceases to be. The brightness of a star extinguished millions of years ago still wanders in the ether where our eyes will perhaps behold it this very night, pursuing its endless road. It is the same with all that we see, as it is with all that we do not see.

The Path to the Mysteries for the purpose of our journey will emerge from the depths of the ocean, and trace its course back along the river valley to the mountain stream beyond...

The Journey Starts Here...

The important thing to realise when we start out on our quest is that every witch who has gone before will have undergone the same experiences and feelings ... and those who have not, will have no understanding of why we want to pursue this new direction of mystical discovery.

One of the issues raised in *Exploring Spirituality* is that the biggest mistake we make is assuming that those closest to us will understand and respect the reasons behind our mystical dissatisfaction and unrest. We take the attitude that if they really felt the same about spiritual development they wouldn't interfere in what we want to do with our own mystical lives. In reality they don't! By changing our perspective in the pursuit of mystical development our fellow witches often interpret this as a rejection of them, their 'truths', beliefs and practices.

It is important for the seeker to accept that any change of either the inner personality or our outer actions, *do* and *will* affect those with whom we've worked magically. There is a noticeable change in outlook (the new ethics we choose to adopt); upon the calls on our time (meetings or ritual observance); and how we deal with personal interaction within the coven (relationships). While we are going through this metamorphosis our fellow witches may struggle to keep up with our newly emerging persona – and it is difficult for them not to feel excluded or left behind. All this will cause a re-evaluation of our relationship within the group, and we will more than likely a) decide it is time to move on, or b) be told that we are no longer considered to be a member of that group.

I still have in my possession a letter from Evan John Jones dating from July 2000 in reply to a query of mine, which goes a long way in explaining how normal this 'wanting to move on' is amongst traditional witches:

I wondered how long it will be before someone asked the question of where Robert [Cochrane] would have been led to in the next step of his magical argosy? I've a very shrewd suspicion having more or less followed in his footsteps and eventually finding myself in more or less the same position as he was. The surprising thing is, it can in many ways lead to a break with his traditional craft and eventually leads on to a highly individual form of devotional workings that in one sense, reverses everything Tubal Cain has to teach. In a sense, you belong yet not belong. You break away from being a member of the group as such and embark on a highly individual way of working yet at the same time, you remain rooted to the clan tradition and the other oddity is, you never actually pass on anything in the sense of the working techniques.

Instead, people have to eventually find their own way there and develop their own particular mystical bent and experiences. Roy once said that Tubal Cain should not be the be-all and end-all of a person's craft experience as each one of us should be capable of reaching far beyond that. The more I think about it, the more I feel he was right, none of us should be led by the hand all our occult lives; we should be free to reach out and find our own spiritual reality without destroying our craft roots. Something so many people fail to grasp and taking the attitude that, 'If you're not with us … then you're against us.' I suppose they hate to lose what they think of as control over the followers.

And just as we cannot control the sea, so we come to realise in our pursuit of the Mysteries, the sea continues to represent that uncontrollable and eternal cycle of life and death, resurrection and re-birth. We see the ocean in terms of the Blessed Isles of the West in death, and also in the concept of the regenerating Waters of Life in the East. Since it is not possible for us to follow this mystical quest from the depths of the ocean and into the air, we must take an alternative route and retrace our footsteps back from the sea and onto the shoreline, along the estuary, and back up the river until we reach its source. There is, of course, a very valid purpose in this exercise which is best summed up in those immortal lines from T S Eliot's *Little Gidding* ...

What we call the beginning is often the end
And to make an end is to make a beginning.
The end is where we start from ...

... And at the end of all our exploring
Will be to arrive where we started
And know the place for the first time ...

In going back over this old ground, some of which we haven't revisited since we were young, eager witchlets, we *will* see things through different eyes. Not through the eyes of a guide or companion pointing out Nature's mystical wonders to a beginner, but as a solitary, mature witch seeking new under-standing of the basic witch-lore we learned so many years ago. The sea, which we thought of as our 'end' becomes our new beginning, and from where we begin the return to where we started our original journey.

So there we have it: the Path to the Mysteries is one we travel alone. We break away from being a member of a group and embark on a highly individual way of working yet at the same time, remaining rooted to our Tradition. We take this knowledge and experience with us, but the trials and tribula-tions we will undergo in the future will be of a completely

different kind to that of group working. Once we embark on our quest there is no turning back and retracing our footsteps...

Try This Exercise:

There is an old adage in transpersonal circles that you cannot change anything but yourself but, in changing yourself, you will find the world changes around you. To effect those changes, however, we first need to know ourselves – and that step is often the most frightening because many of us don't want to face those facets of our personality or character that lurk in the shadows. Here you need to consider three points and record your reaction in a special mystical journal:

- What do you do when faced with two or more conflicting truths?
- Do you seek to avoid problems or overcome them?
- Do you accumulate information and the benefit of other people's experience in preparation for a possible need, or do you wait for a circumstance to occur before acquiring the relevant information?

Learning to explore our own spirituality enables us to realise that truth is subjective, *according to where we are standing at the precise moment at which we pose the question* – and what appears as inspiration to one person, will be completely incomprehensible to another.

Chapter Two

Between Land and Sea (Water Margin)

*Mystery: [Prob from A-F misterie, OF mistere, (F mystère) L
mysterium, Gr musterion] Something beyond human comprehension;
a secret or obscure matter; a divine truth only partially revealed.*
[*The Waverley Modern English Dictionary*]

For the traditional witch, the shoreline represents the primordial
meeting place of the Elements of Earth and Water in all its guises,
from the gentle interchanges of tides and salt marshes to the
brutal confrontation of waves and rocky sea cliffs. We come to
understand that the shoreline is a place of timeless transformation, where grains of sand and huge slabs of cliff-face are at
the mercy of the seas that erode them with the surge of every
tide. The sediments that have been carried to the shore by inland
rivers are swept along the coast by swirling currents and
deposited elsewhere by the relentless surf.

The Buddha described the experience of enlightenment as 'a
drop of water merging with the sea from which it came'; other
mystics who have stood on the shoreline and meditated on the
vast expanse of ocean stretching to the horizon, have also
reflected upon this thought. When we stand at the water margin
we are symbolically pulling ourselves out of the primordial sea
to begin this solitary journey across the landscape to complete
the cycle and rejoin the water from the sea, where it falls as rain
on the mountainside. Our quest will throw up obstacles that we
must overcome *without* the help of others, and although this may
prove harder, it will give far more personal satisfaction and a
sense of achievement in the long run.

The famous 'dark night of the soul' is not a myth, as many
witches who have undergone the trial themselves will testify,

and everyone on a mystical journey will, sooner or later, need to cross this dark river. It symbolises a passage between two states, or levels of awareness, and the crossing represents an acceptance of the dangers and sacrifices to be encountered on the Path we are seeking on our quest. It will certainly be a different approach to our familiar 'coven' or 'solitary' Craft – and it will be a completely strange and unfamiliar road.

Exploring Spirituality included a quote from psychotherapist and mystic, Anny Wyse, who explained that there comes a time when the seeker takes the '...traditional 'leap into the void'. Where one let go of all the safety harnesses of training, text books, supervisors and other people's approval and says 'It is so!' Once that moment has been achieved one has a new perspective on life, the Universe and everything.' And there was more to come:

> One does, however, have to put up with the disapproval of one's erstwhile friends and colleagues [fellow witches and coveners]. Ian Gordon-Brown used an interesting image in his workshop *Initiation*. This was that we work or live within one circle of people, jobs, etc., until we discover it is too small to contain us any longer. We have to cross its boundary into a larger, more inclusive world and it is likely that few, if any, of our friends want to come with us. They may well try to stop us leaving, argue that we are 'wrong'. We have to choose – stay and suffocate, or go on and be lonely, scared, clumsy, unknowing. Sooner or later we choose to move on...

The Path of an Old Craft witch is littered with lost friendships and acquaintances, many of whom were considered to be our closest comrades at one time. People whom we trusted implicitly, but for whatever reason for the relationship ending, there was probably a magical or mystical purpose that was hidden from us at that point in time. It may be that our Guardian felt that the continuation of a particular relationship would be detrimental to our own personal magical-mystical development and, like a watchful parent, decided to throw a spanner in the works. We may view this as a warning and decide that the price is too great, but as every magical practitioner knows, there is *always* a price.

So, standing here at the water margin, we need to contemplate what it is we are searching for before we stride over the sand towards our new-found spiritual freedom. Our witchcraft has taught us the basic tenets of belief and that traditional British Old Craft like those ancient mysteries of Egypt; the ancestral beliefs of Japanese Shinto; the Aboriginal tribes of Australia; and the indigenous Native Americans, is fundamentally animistic. It may appear far-fetched to compare British Old Craft with ancient Egyptian belief, but this fact was acknowledged by Egyptologist Rosalie David in her introduction to *Egyptian Magic* by Christian Jacq.

In ancient Egypt … all elements of life, whether human-beings, animals, or even gods, were considered to be animated by a spiritual force which could be manipulated and it was thought that all inanimate objects were also imbued with magical power. Essentially, the spiritual and material were believed to be woven from the same substance, and it was considered possible, by using magic to control the order of the cosmos and to modify individual destiny by combating negative trends...

Animism is, of course, the belief that every object, animate and inanimate, has its own life-force, or energy. Here there is no separation between the spiritual or physical world, where 'spirit' exists in all flora and fauna (including humans), rocks, geological features such as mountains, rivers and springs; and in natural phenomena such as storms, wind and the movement of heavenly bodies. It is the understanding that a small quartz pebble can link us with the cosmic Divine.

These were the lessons taught by Bob and Mériém Clay-Egerton in the Coven of the Scales. That it wasn't necessary to rely on ritual, Circle casting, chanting and dancing to generate magical energy because it is there, all around us on a permanent basis. It means that a natural witch can be on her contacts in seconds; knowing what type of energy, or witch-power is needed to cure a headache, or channel the strength to walk the death-path with confidence after being diagnosed with a terminal illness. It really is a belief that can move mountains – if the application is right – and all witches draw on this 'witch-power' to cause change through the application of Will. This power is similar to the energy raised by *tai chi* – and *tai chi* is widely used within art and sport without any magical significance whatsoever. In other words, it is a perfectly natural energy or force that can be harnessed or tapped into on a daily basis to a greater or lesser extent.

But what does a witch hold to be the three basic beliefs?

1. That there is one originating 'force'
2. That this force is completely natural
3. That this natural force can be used by mankind

What does a witch ask for?

1. Sufficient nourishment (food and/or knowledge)
2. Shelter from the elements (also with a hidden meaning)
3. Love (again with hidden meaning)

What does a witch seek?

1. Knowledge, plus wisdom, plus understanding
2. Belief in tolerance and balance
3. The rule of natural law

It has also been said that a witch has three hearts. One is a false heart for all the world to see; an inner heart to show to family and very special friends and the real heart, the true one, the secret one, which is known only to him/herself. Generations of witches have learned to disappear within themselves. We grow impenetrable walls behind which we live, helped by rituals and customs to cleanse our mind of people, and put ourselves onto a different plane. Sunset watching is a great help or listening to the rain: have you noticed the different sounds of rain? Or the noise made by a breeze through the leaves of the trees? Listening and watching are exceptionally good exercises to induce harmony; they are messages to our centre, to remind us of the transience of life, to help us gain harmony; to escape from stress and suddenly be a million miles away, safe and alone.

Remembering these things, as we stand on this metaphorical water margin in the knowledge that we are about to take our leave of all that is comforting and secure, it is right and proper that there should be a degree of trepidation. As *Traditional Witchcraft for the Seashore* reflects, it is here we are consciously aware that although the land and sea are governed by their own supernatural lore, the narrow margin between them has long been considered a gateway to Otherworld, and as such, is a dangerous place to be. In passing from the Element of Water to the Element of Earth, the seeker would need to act appropriately. Patterns in the sand created by the receding tide can be used for divination where slight depressions are caused by water gouging out some sand as it flows back to the sea. The sand is deposited a little further down the beach to form a variety of patterns; clusters of empty shells can also be used *in situ* as divinatory tools. Ask your question and see what impressions you get from these natural phenomena.

Because we are about to start living by the pull of natural tides and symbols instead of a date on a calendar, we would be well advised to put *all* magical equipment and regalia away for the time being. There is no place for these baubles on the Path to the Mysteries, although few witches will be separated from their knife and cord, which act as symbolic weapons of defence and a statement of intent linked to the witch's Oath. The further along the Path we travel the more heightened our senses to the messages coming in on the breeze and for the urban dweller *'even in the city's throng I feel the freshness of the streams'*. We know, for example, that the sea is in constant motion and as *Secrets of the Seashore* observes:

> This is obvious enough on a rough day when the wind has whipped up waves which pound and roar on the beach; but even during calm periods, when hardly a ripple disturbs the surface, great masses of water are being shifted around the coast by tidal currents governed by the phases of the moon. As the water moves, so it transports any material that is floating or in suspension without any independent means of propulsion.

The witch must also be aware that there all manner of other different currents and movements on the planet that affect us on a deeper magico-mystical level. Let us consider for a moment Professor Brian Cox's comment that every blade of grass has 3.8 billion years of history written into it. Or what we often blithely refer to as 'Earth Mysteries', which can produce a mild tingling sensation; set the pendulum swinging; or a burst of warm energy in our hands and feet. But do we stop to think that this could be caused by the swirling molten layer under the Earth's crust, creating the electro-magnetic field that surrounds the planet by the spinning outer crust around the solid part of the inner core? Or is our Elemental Earth just a quiet ramble in the countryside and a container of sand marking the Northern quarter?

We may sit meditating by a rippling stream, watching the sunlight dance in the water as it trips over the stones and pebbles in its path – but do we allow our minds to explore the greater picture of where that crystal clear water comes from? Do we realise that this stream began its brief chapter of life being drawn up as vapour from the ocean and falling as rain on the hills and mountain sides, before flowing down into the river valley with enough power to bring rocks and stones tumbling in its wake? Do our magical energies focus on the stream; the rainfall on the mountain; or the ocean? Are we constantly aware of the force of that water-flow throughout the seasons – the spring floods; the summer drought; the clogging of the channel with autumn leaves and the frozen surface in winter. Or does our concept of Elemental Water begin and end with the symbolic bowl of tap water marking the Western quarter in our magic Circle?

Nothing on the planet can live without clean, breathable air, but the witch needs to think beyond soft summer breezes and rainbows after a spring shower. Air is the stuff from which tornadoes and hurricanes are made; it brings puffs of cumulus clouds or a billowing thunderhead some 10 miles high; not to mention the thousands-of-feet-high dust storms that are created when a monsoon collides with dry air currents above it. Or is our Elemental Air merely the smoke from a perfumed joss stick marking the Eastern quarter in our magical workings?

Fire, even in its most modest form has the capacity for destruction – a box of matches in the hands of a child, a fallen candle, or a carelessly discarded cigarette. On a grander and more epic scale, we are well acquainted by television coverage with devastating wildfire destroying anything that stands in its path; the eruption of a volcano; or the power of solar winds that reach out from the sun to interfere with electronic equipment here on Earth. Or is our contact with Elemental Fire restricted to a candle burning at the Southern quarter of our Circle?

As the currents and tides of Elemental Earth, Water, Air and Fire move around on our higher level of consciousness, we must take the opportunity to examine the 'material' that is floating around or 'in suspension without any independent means of propulsion' on a more mystical level. Take for example sight of the famous 'green ray' so loved by the mystics, and often written about by those who have never seen it. While we remain at the edge of the sea we are in the most advantageous place to catch a glimpse of it – if we are lucky. A glimpse of the green ray, however, is not there for the asking. From a scientific viewpoint, this natural phenomenon is caused by refraction: a vertical spectrum of colours that seems to sink below the horizon with the setting sun – red first. Because blue is scattered by the air and lost, green – one of the last colours in the sequence – sometimes can take on a fleeting brilliance.

Professor of physics and astronomy, Chet Raymo, knows exactly under what conditions the green ray *should* appear and has pursued it throughout his life since first reading about it in a scientific paper in 1965.

The green flash turned out to be grandly evasive; thirty years later, I am still waiting and watching ... I have seen my share of lights in the sky. I have seen the aurora borealis and the zodiacal light. I have seen sun dogs and rings around the moon. I have seen double and even triple rainbows. I have seen the midnight sun. But I have not seen the green flash.

Scientific interest in the phenomenon has its origins in a work of science fiction of Jules Verne's *Le Rayon Vert*, published in 1882 and referred to by occultists ever since. For a long time it was considered to be an optical illusion until science proved it otherwise. Despite a scientific background, Raymo also has the soul of a poet and muses that: 'The flash if obtained, will be like a signal from out there in the sea of mystery, a signature of the Absolute, a spectral revelation.' Perhaps this is why occultists value its brief glimpse; that we are only given this rarest of Nature's gifts if we happen to be receptive at that particular point in time. I have seen it but once – as the sun sank behind the

Prescelli Mountains in West Wales and disappeared into the sea. The green ray exists – it is *not* a trick of the retina.

Similarly, the term 'enlightenment' has been bandied around for many years now, to such a degree that it has become almost meaningless in the West. Nevertheless, enlightenment is what we are seeking. When it comes to enlightenment, like the green ray, we cannot control the circumstances under which we receive it because it is not something we can create for ourselves. Although self-discipline allows us to control the effect and the aftermath of the experience – we have no control over the timing and 'quality' of the experience itself. Neither would it be wise to count one blinding flash of inspiration or guidance as enlightenment. In this case, Zen philosophy offers a good example of what we should look for when it comes to understanding the differences in the variety of experiences that come our way on the Path to the Mysteries. We should never fool ourselves that we've had a full mind-blowing experience when, in fact, we've only registered one on the mystical Richter scale.

Satori is the Zen term used to describe a state of consciousness beyond the plain of discrimination. It means 'the first showing'. This experience may vary in quality and duration from a flash of intuitive awareness to Nirvana (the limitations of existence). It is the *beginning* and not the end of our Path to the Mysteries; it may be far removed from enlightenment in terms of long years of training. *Kensho*, which means 'seeing into one's own nature', is the goal of Zen practice and the first experience of *satori*. In other words, we will undergo a series of mini-enlightenments before we hit the big time; and even then we've still got a long way to go.

Whatever it is that we experience, however, must be put into perspective. Unless we put our hearts and minds in order and asked ourselves all the pertinent questions in coming to terms with our personal weaknesses, we cannot expect successful Initiation into the Mysteries. The following are traditional qualities expected in any seeker of the Mysteries and are equally applicable for the traditional witch. We must:

- Want to attain 'it' whatever we perceive 'it' to be.
- Possess humility that is consistent with a will to succeed.
- Accept that 'faith' will be tested over and over again.
- Have a mind of our own and a measure of control over it.
- Be profoundly aware of the limits of the intellect.
- Possess a well-balanced mind that will not buckle under the strain.
- Have an innate feeling for the Path we have chosen.

In view of the dearth of established written spiritual guidelines for Craft protocols on a deeper/higher level, I have often resorted to classic Zen and Shinto teaching as examples, simply because they are the closest historical precedents we have to traditional witchcraft, and a discipline that played an important part in my own formative years. Shinto has survived for hundreds of years and is older than Christianity, and yet it should not be considered an old 'pagan' belief in respecting and revering the traditions of the past as the 'Way of the Gods'. Perhaps, as the authors of *The Great Religions* suggest, many of the religious answers of the old 'spirit of Japan' remain a force to consider in the world today. They also suggest that others might find similar satisfaction through simply attempting life as it is and appreciating it for the beauties and wonders it offers the person who takes time to see and hear.

The Journey Continues...

The shore remains a place of compromise, conflict and eternal change – which are the elements of thought that mark this part of our journey. *Traditional Witchcraft for the Seashore* explored the importance of working with natural tides instead of the 'traditional' pagan dates marked out with depressing regularity on the

Gregorian calendar and from now on we will be governed by Nature's tides alone...

Looking Back

The coastal landscape we are leaving behind is a result of the constant changes in sea level, caused by fluctuations in ocean currents, by the drifting of tectonic plates, or by the sudden shift of the Earth's crust. All these upheavals are mirrored in the stresses and pressures we've faced in our personal and magical lives, and which we now leave behind like flotsam and jetsam at the high-water line. Of course there will be regrets, but if we embark on a mystical quest then we cannot afford the luxury of baggage, no matter how fondly we cling to the past.

Looking Forward

As we walk away from the shoreline it is important to realise that there is a long way to go before we are free of the tang of the briny ocean and that the landscape over which we now travel is full of the hidden dangers of mud flats, salt marshes and quicksand. Depending on the strength of the currents along the coast, it may also take many months or even years for the heavier brine of the sea to absorb the lighter and less dense river water into the open ocean. We can leave the sea behind but it will be a long time before we are free of its influence in terms of tidal reaches and salt-sea breezes; just the same as in freeing ourselves from the long reach of our past life. In leaving the past behind, we must also be wary of the perils that may lie ahead in terms of new acquaintances on our mystical Path.

Beware False Prophets

Whatever Path we tread, however, there must be some form of guidance and on a mystical level this will often appear in the unexpected arrival of a mentor or teacher. An initial reaction may be that we feel we don't need anyone to mediate between ourselves and the Powers That Be. Of course we don't *need* anyone – but how can anyone explore a hidden Path when we may not know its pitfalls and dangers, or what the quest ultimately entails? How can we teach ourselves what we don't know exists? This is the type of instruction that cannot be found in books, especially the kind that extol the virtues of working with angels, orbs and flower fairies.

There's also that old adage in esoteric circles that we will discover our next teacher when we are ready to receive the wisdom they are willing to bestow on us. Nevertheless, despite the desire to pursue the mystical quest under the guidance of someone more experienced, the seeker will often find it necessary to rely on our own resources via:

- Acting on knowledge already received.
- The wisdom to correctly interpret intuition and instinct.
- The understanding of what the message refers to at this *precise moment in time*.

It is often when we are in this state of mystical limbo that we can fall prey to unscrupulous gurus who hover on the periphery of the seeker's vision, whispering from the shadows. Because we become desperate for more mystical experiences it is easy to become tempted by those who claim to be able to help us along the Path – if only we'll just step down this side road. More often than not this type of diversion ends in tears and recriminations because at this stage of our journey we are more vulnerable than we have ever been. We *want* to believe; we *want* to experience – and we're willing to follow anyone who promises to show us the way. At this point a seeker becomes lost in a series of one-way systems and blind alleys to such a degree that they either settle for second best or give up the quest altogether. This is where we find that our fellow travellers fall into several different categories.

- Those who are looking for a mentor who will tell them what to do. Often they tarry a while hoping to find what they haven't been able to with other teachers.
- Those who seize upon anything new in order to be different amongst their existing group. They play with it for a while and then follow the next fad because they don't want to put in the hard work necessary for a true mystical quest.
- Those who are desperately seeking that indefinable *something* to fill their lives. Often they're looking for a 'new set of rules' to apply to their daily routine and will experiment with anything that appears 'mystical' to them.
- Those who embrace the quest on a physical or superficial level. They want the results without putting in the effort to acquire genuine knowledge.
- Those who from the very first introduction know that this is what they've always wanted. This is what they *are*. They no longer need to follow the Path, the Path has found them. They have become the Path.

By this stage on our journey we will have already realised that we cannot seek out the Mysteries by reading books and remaining casual observers. The time for play-acting is over and we must seriously accept that unless we allow that divine spark to ignite our soul (psyche or inner self), then we will remain spiritual tourists – the time has come for assuming responsibility for our future actions.

There is an old Zen saying that to walk the Path is to become the Path; in other words: 'When the pupil is ready, the Master appears.' This obviously implies that the seeker must advance by his or her own efforts before they need, or have 'earned' the physical presence of a teacher – in whatever guise they appear. Nevertheless, as we begin the journey inland and leave the shore behind, we will almost certainly be travelling alone.

Try This Exercise:

Much of what we read today in pagan books and magazines over-simplifies the pursuit of spiritual development by trivialising it for the mass-consumer market. If we believe what we read in such publications, we can come away with the impression that our hidden spiritual self can be discovered on the shelf at the supermarket and paid for by credit card.

The first thing we do is to redefine our own natural energies. Forget about the neo-pagan maid, mother, crone elements of the lunar cycle and see the natural tides as they really are within Nature. As strange as it may seem, this will help you to keep track of the tidal ebb and flow on both the inner and outer levels, because here we are working on Simon Baron-Cohen's theory of the male brain being hard-wired for understanding and systemising; the female brain for empathising and sympathising. Begin by recording the actual phases of the moon and the corresponding tides and how they affect your personal witch-power – for example:

New Moon	Spring Tide*	Lunar Pull	Female
First Quarter	Neap Tide	Solar Pull	Male
Full Moon	Spring Tide*	Lunar Pull	Female
Third Quarter	Neap Tide	Solar Pull	Male

* *Spring Tide does not refer to the season but the phase of the moon*

Although systemising (male brain) and empathising (female brain) are wholly different processes, we *all* have both skills. The question is: how much of each have *you* got? Baron-Cohen's theory expands to inform us that not all men have 'male' brains, and not all females have 'female' brains – the 'hunting gene' for example, can be equally as strong in both male and female, while the caring professions attract large numbers of males. Similarly, male and female Mysteries are different – and yet still highly compatible.

Here we come up against the law of opposites that are so important in esoteric practice: light/dark, night/day, active/passive, negative/positive, etc. One cannot exist without the other to act as a measuring stick – and so it is with male and female energies on a magico-mystical level. To walk the Path to the Mysteries successfully, we need to learn to see situations from both sides, to allow that both male and female have equally valid viewpoints concerning life, to flow with both solar and lunar tides. For example:

When looking at a mountain, do you think about how precisely it was formed, or view it as just part of a magnificent landscape?

- When walking in the country are you aware of how the various trees differ, or just think of it as a pleasant place to pass the time in a relaxing setting?
- Are you interested in knowing the path a river takes from its source to the sea, or considering the levels of pollution in the water?
- Are you curious about life on other planets, or feel that it is a too vast an issue to contemplate?

Here we need to school ourselves into constantly thinking beyond the obvious so that we have no boundaries to our imagination – to both systemise *and* empathise. We instinctively come to *know* that mountains are continuously reshaping; that trees are part of the lifecycle of decay and regeneration; that rivers are the life-giving arteries of the landscape; and that life in some form does exist on other planets somewhere in the galaxy. And even more importantly, that gender is *unimportant* to a witch on a mystical quest.

Chapter Three

The Personal Universe (Estuary)

Mysteries: A kind of medieval drama, the characters and events of which were drawn from sacred history.
[*Brewer's Dictionary of Phrase & Fable*]

An Old Craft witch sees the estuary as being neither river nor sea, but as something in between. It is a body of water whose composition is an ever-shifting mix of fresh water from continental rivers and salt water from the ocean. The estuary is also the place of myth and legend, from drowned river valleys to submerged lost kingdoms and re-emerging wetlands. That is not to mention maritime wonder when ocean-going mariners discovered that anchoring in the fresh waters at the upper end of an estuary could kill several months' accumulation of barnacles on a ship's hull!

In *Traditional Witchcraft for the Seashore* a great deal was made of the magical energies of the estuary, and it can be described as a battleground where salt sea and fresh-water river fight for supremacy, with final victory denied to both due to the wide variations in the salinity, temperature and sediment content. The salinity of an estuary ranges across the widest possible spectrum – from fresh water in its upper reaches to sea water at its lowest end where the concentration changes from hour to hour, from place to place and from depth to depth.

At this new stage of our mystical quest we continue to alter our perspectives and accept that we are trying to define something intangible in tangible terms. Learning to know ourselves is essential in order to develop our mystic awareness, but any lack of introspection shouldn't stop us from making a start on the journey. Every step taken from now on will be directed towards the mystical goal – whatever, whenever and wherever it turns out to be. We must remember not to take things we read or hear too literally, since it is difficult to talk about mystical matters on a mundane level and so the language hovers precariously between the obtuse and mystical vagueness. Neither should things be taken too seriously since we can easily become bogged down with pseudo-mysticism that can be extremely confusing for the seeker. The witch often has only intuition to fall back on – that and the guidance of the Ancestors as we begin to confront our own 'personal universe'.

The multi-facets of the estuary reflect the wide variety of different planes that we discover when encountering our own personal Universe and we quickly learn to develop the art of perspective; to look on things at a deeper level, but without being too analytical. For example, any classical painting is executed according to the laws of perspective. What this means is that the images the artist has painted smaller, the viewer feels are further away and insignificant; images painted larger appear to be nearer and more prominent. The artist can make us feel that we are floating up in the air looking down on a subject; or in a valley looking upwards; or in any direction he chooses. The artist has chosen the direction from which we will view the subject, forcing us to look with *his eyes – from his perspective*. Once we begin our mystical quest, however, this is the last time we will ever view any part of the Universe from someone else's perspective, because the whole of the Universe can only be seen by us, from wherever we happen to be.

There is an old Celtic riddle that asks: 'Where is the centre of the Universe?' and the answer is always 'Here!' because *everything* we observe is seen from our own personal viewpoint – and we are not just talking about the way we use our eyes. We begin to put our personal slant on everything we observe or experience; we all react differently and interpret the world around us from differing viewpoints. When we begin to move into different realms of thought, however, the signposts we've relied on in the past get fewer and further between. The meanings become more fluid, more open to interpretation. This is especially so when we come into areas concerned with personal belief. This is where the feeling that we are isolated in a strange personal Universe can become too much for some; they feel safer with the herd where the signposts are clear-cut and tangible.

When a witch starts to explore a more personal form of *mystical* development, the signposts become even more 'iffy' and those who try to help can only give hints and tips on finding our way. This may give the appearance of being evasive, but in reality they are simply confirming that no one but *you* can interpret your personal Universe. As Michael Howard has observed, most Old Crafters have a 'trickster' aspect to their character and personality and for that reason, a lot of what we are told has to be taken with a large degree of circumspection. We also have to accept that there is no one way by which we can achieve mystical enlightenment; even the most experienced teacher can only point the seeker in the right direction. At this stage we discover that there are two clear stages of mystical development ahead of us:

- The journey to the Gateway of our true Path;
- And the travelling along the Path itself.

Many seekers find it difficult to accept that it may be a long road ahead before we even reach that Gateway! In mystical terms this is the 'gate of conversion' – the spiritual point of no return. Before we reach this point, however, we must have learned how to know ourselves – the first rule of Old Craft – or we wouldn't be standing here. This is where an understanding of the *kensho* and *satori* experiences enable us to see what a short way we've travelled and not fool ourselves into believing that we have arrived – and this can be a very humbling experience indeed.

To return to a Zen analogy of this stage of our journey: this reveals the seeker stumbling blindly through the gloom of his or her own ignorance (and inexperience) to find the Gate. 'Initiation into the mysteries of the way needs no divine initiator save as we choose to project that concept out of the human mind,' wrote one such anonymous Master. 'We test ourselves, or are tested by our own past *karma*; we succeed in or we fail that test – and it may be that we shall fail it again and again. Then suddenly ... we are on the way, and thereafter there is but one command, walk on!'

The quest will now be unceasing and the first experiences will, more often than not, be unpleasant, regardless of whichever Path (or Tradition) we follow. We must get to grips with this realisation so that there are no nasty surprises to be discovered later on. We will find ourselves stepping from a well-worn track into a fog that conceals quicksand, sheer rock and apparently inhospitable wilderness. We must learn to walk on and observe that which was previously hidden. Though we may receive guidance and encouragement from a teacher, *we must walk on alone*. Mystical development is something that happens to an individual when the scales begin to fall from the seeker's eyes, and the world is perceived in a different light. It doesn't matter whether we are male or female, young or old, there is no restriction on our perception because this 'something' is neither ageist or sexist. No matter how we decide to express this pursuit of the inconceivable, we have to accept responsibility for our own actions and the repercussions.

For the witch who finds these ideas unpalatable, the mystical quest will probably shudder to a halt. We can retrace our steps back to safety, but the damage is already done. The 'innocence' of thought that kept us happily immersed in coven ritual and relationships will have already evaporated. We have already come too far to regain that blissful state of ignorance, so although we may *physically* abandon the quest, the permanent damage done to us on an emotional and mental level is immeasurable. The scars will never fully heal.

Anima Mundi – The Soul of the World

One major difficulty with mystical experiences is how we sort the genuine from self-delusion. At least some of the responses will be nothing more than a product of our own brain indulging in a little fantasy – how do we tell?

Esoteric matters have to do with the hidden, often deliberately concealed, truths that can be grasped only through intuition or revelation that elude any and all experimental verification. The esoteric is a way of thinking unto itself, irrational and intuitive, aimed at the 'overarching unity of nature' and the correspondences within it. It lives in the magic of the mysterious, a higher state of consciousness that remains closed to those who have not been tempted into following the Mystery Path. And it would only be natural to question the existence of 'God' in the process. Perhaps some of the best advice, however, comes from philosopher and Roman Emperor, Marcus Aurelius in his *Meditations*:

> To them that ask thee, where has thou seen the Gods, or how knowest thou certainly that there be Gods, that thou art so devout in their worship? I answer first of all, that even to the very eye, they are in some manner visible and apparent. Secondly, neither have I ever seene mine own soule, and yet I respect and honour it. So then for the Gods, by the dayly experience that I have of their power and providence towards my selfe and others, I know certainly that they are, and therefore worship them.

In *Exploring Spirituality*, transpersonal psychologist and shaman Anny Wyse observed that when the mind starts reaching beyond the current 'known', the psyche is activated and can begin to spin threads outwards from the self to other parts of 'Otherworld'.

> The level on which these things (beings, images) become real is the place where we can leap beyond the fences and hedges

and prison bars of 'normal'. Otherworld is real all the time and everywhere but we have to take our distorting and reducing lenses off in order to see it. And it has nothing to do with belief – although belief can be the first stepping stone to knowing. As Jung said: 'I don't believe! I know!' And so do all mystics.

As witches will already understand, these archetypal beings belong to the realm of Otherworld – the Anima Mundi – and derive from *arche* and *typos*, two Greek words put together to try to give imaginable shape and form to the 'Gods'. 'The word 'archetype' gives a respectable protection from the enormity of the concept of godhead,' Anny Wyse continued.

If one uses the word 'god' it can become frighteningly up-close and personal. For the Gods are real and exist outside of, beyond, and despite us. Perhaps this is some of the difficulty. If we have Gods then we may find ourselves insignificantly small in the great scheme of things. Most people don't have a sufficiently integrated and secure ego to be able to accept this with equanimity. But the Gods are there. Otherworld is there. And here.

The *anima*, or the world soul, is an ethereal spirit that is diffused throughout all of Nature; and just as every human has a physical body and a soul, so the world is a living organism with a soul. According to several systems of thought, it is an intrinsic connection between all living things on the planet, which relates to our world in much the same way as the soul is connected to the human body. The idea originated with Plato, whereby this world is a living being endowed with a soul and intelligence ... a single visible living entity containing all other living entities, which by their nature are all inter-related.

This state of being results in cosmic consciousness or Jung's theory of collective unconscious; the concept of an interconnected network of consciousness that reaches out through time, with each conscious being linked to every other and therefore the only vital force in the Universe, *and a direct link to the experience of all preceding generations.* The term was introduced by psychiatrist Carl Jung to represent a form of the unconscious common to mankind as a whole, and originating in the inherited structure of the human mind. It is part of racial memory as opposed to the personal unconscious, which arises from the experience of the individual.

According to Jung, the collective unconscious links to the archetypes, or universal primordial (*Anima Mundi*) with those symbols arising spontaneously in radically different cultures because people saw the images in dreams or visions. He held that these sigils and symbols reached beyond personal subconscious memories and drew upon a universal bank of information: universal templates of human behaviour that were the proto-types of all of the mythological and religious symbology of the world. The Qabalah, Tarot and Magical Correspondences are built entirely upon archetypal imagery, hence the importance of a witch (or any magical practitioner) having a clear understanding of what these symbols mean.

The theory of the collective unconscious is compelling in that it could possibly explain many of the experiences people have a hard time coming to terms with, such as regression and past-life experiences that we read about in the mind, body and spirit publications. If in fact, archetypes and the collective unconscious play a significant role in our lives and behaviour, it could in theory, be possible to link this to a kind of psychic animal instinct – which becomes second-nature to an Old Craft witch.

For most people the ability to connect with this level of consciousness is almost impossible, because we have denied its existence for centuries, preferring to believe in previous lives

and reincarnation. Once on the mystical Path, however, we will reconnect with this world of the *Anima Mundi* and see it as another part of our own personal Universe.

The Journey Continues...

In esoteric terms, the estuary can be considered our 'time between times'; that strange, netherworld found at dawn and dusk, where the traditional witch finds it easy to slip into the psychic realms. Here there is a mingling of wonderful images and currents, just like in the estuary where there is a great deal more than just the process of the mingling of sea water and fresh water. We are reminded that because the fresh water is lighter than sea water, river water entering the estuary overrides the salt water and spreads outward toward the sea. When the flow of the river is substantially stronger than the force of the tides, the heavier salt water tends to be pushed down to the estuary floor.

Whatever else an estuary may be, like Otherworld it is never clear-cut and pristine. Unlike a clear mountain stream or the crystalline waters of the Caribbean, an estuary is a soupy cauldron of life – an ecological twilight zone. Otherworld has similar properties that a witch must confront during his or her quest, similar to those other strange intermediate zones at the edge of many seashores and estuaries – being both at the same time aquatic and terrestrial; wetlands, too frequently submerged by tides or flooding to be called land, and too frequently exposed to be considered bodies of water. Like sea water, Otherworld energies reach into all the difference psychic and astral planes:

> Having slipped through inlets, past headlands and open beaches, into embayments and up river entrances, into hundreds of winding creeks and sheltered coves, the sea's final surge of tidal power is spent. It slows on sandy flats, eddies farther inland through expanses of mud and at last eases to a stop amid grassy salt-marshes ... These wetlands

are saturated not only by the tides but by rivers and streams. As the fresh water runoff arrives in the wetlands, its flow is retarded ... providing a self-repairing natural protection against surging storm waves.

Edge of the Sea, Russell Sackett

And finally, if we were to view these estuaries and mud flats from the air, where tidal coverage is shallow, we will often find a classic, tree-shaped pattern – the branches formed from the numerous channels of the naturally created drainage systems. A symbolic Tree of Life with its branches reaching out towards the sea – and its roots spreading far inland towards the source of our journey.

Try This Exercise:

A mystical quest will often challenge many of a witch's precon-ceived ideas about what it is we want to explore. We can often find ourselves changing direction unconsciously or uninten-tionally, as personal values come under the microscope and we are forced to re-examine the rules that have governed our lives. Make a note of the responses to these questions in your mystical journal:

- What does mystical growth mean to you?
- Does it offer a sense of inner peace and harmony?
- Can you feel a sense of the 'divine' in the world around you?
- Which personal values does your mystical quest challenge?
- Are you prepared to meet those challenges?
- Do you want to continue your quest, or remain a bystander?

It may be too soon to answer the questions simply because it means thinking about them. In terms of mystical growth, the intellect can often stifle the natural flow of reflection and/or inner peace. Bear in mind that many highly respected mystics have been simple folk, whose minds were not hindered by the demands of relationships, commerce or intellect.

There should be no sense of failure should you choose not to continue your quest. Even if you feel that an advanced mystical approach to life is not for you, perhaps your perceptions have expanded a little to allow you to look on life around you with a greater understanding. If this is the case, then you have not failed in your intent.

Chapter Four

Ancestors and Ritual Landscape
(Still Water)

Mystic: [Of mystique, L mysticus, Gr mustikos] Pertaining to or involving mystery or mysticism; occult; esoteric; allegorical; emblematical; one addicted to mysticism; a supporter of the doctrine of mysticism.
[*The Waverley Modern English Dictionary*]

As the witch's mystical inner self begins to assert its influence over how we perceive the world around us, we become more and more attuned to the *genius loci*, the particular character, influence, or association of a place which is often described as the spirit guardian. It doesn't matter if it's natural or man-created, a voice calls to us from within and creates a special bond even if the moment is as fleeting as sunlight on water.

For the traditional witch, however, this should be familiar territory since many folk have come to Old Craft via an interest in what we call 'Earth Mysteries' – and what we can liken to the still waters found in different locations of lowland ponds and marshes where our early Ancestors lived.

It is a well-known fact to archaeologists and anthropologists that a lot of indigenous settlements were created around still water and at this stage of the hunter-gatherer's development the witch finds early indications of what later became incorporated into Craft practice. Recent archaeological findings have revealed a great deal about the beliefs of these early settlers and a large number of important artefacts have come to light from the still water of our ponds and marshes. Archaeologist Francis Pryor [*Britain BC*] says that the abundance is far greater than can be accounted for in accidental loss, and points towards votive offerings made at the water's edge and the veneration these early people had for watery places.

Here, by the still water we need to tarry a while and reflect on our ancestry and heritage – and most importantly, what it means to be a witch; and what effect our location has upon us – on both the inner and outer planes. By regulating our own 'calendar' in tune with the natural tides and seasons we integrate our most inner feelings to what is going on around us without having to think about it, since we register these changes on a much more subliminal level. Our mystical world of still water reflects that of Nature in that each water habitat is different although most consist of a deeper layer, little disturbed by the vagaries of the weather above; the shallows, and the all-important margin where land and water meet – making the best use of both worlds.

We also become aware that regardless of where we live in the world, some geological formations are better suited for magical or creative working than others, an idea that was mooted by Dion Fortune in her novel, *The Goat-Foot God*. ... 'Now the best place to get the kind of experiences you want is on chalk. If you think of it, all the earliest civilisation in these islands was on the chalk ... Avebury's on the chalk; and St Albans is on the chalk ...'

Christopher Tilley in *A Phenomenology of Landscape*, however, gives a wider overview of the topographic features of the prehistoric landscape that attracted our distant Ancestors' attention: an affinity with the coast; mountain escarpments and spurs; the ridges, valleys and chalk downlands. Obviously, the most important aspect of each site being not what is seen above ground, but the geological formation beneath our feet.

There are, of course, many different types of rock that make up the Earth's surface and each of them will have certain positive or negative magical/creative properties. As an example, we will look at what has been found from personal experience to be the best and the worst when it comes to drawing from, or stifling magical/creative energy.

The Best

Slate is a widespread, metamorphic rock commonly found inter-layered with sedimentary strata and with rocks of volcanic origin. Once we understand that *quartz* is very abundant in slate and may form as much as 70 percent by weight of the rock, it is not difficult to see why this particular material generates so much Earth energy – quartz being one of the most powerful crystals on the planet. Magical, psychic and creative working on slate packs a very distinctive punch, especially if the slate layers are close to the surface.

The Worst

Clay – the name derives from Old English *clæg* meaning 'sticky' – is a widespread sedimentary rock with grains too small to be seen under any but the most powerful microscope, and may form in many different geological environments throughout the world. The most extensive layers are found in both deep and shallow marine deposits, in moraines (piles of debris) left behind by receding glaciers, and in zones of pre-existent rocks (especially granite) that have been altered by hydrothermal fluids. Try walking through heavy clay and it immediately becomes apparent why Earth energy is often 'blocked' or sluggish. Magical working on clay involves a lot of energy-generating techniques by the practitioner, and unless there is a considerable amount of experience (and knowledge) to draw on, things may take a long time to come to fruition.

Personal Level

Even here we must seek out which energies work for us on a *personal* level, and on this very personal journey we will be experiencing anew the locations that suit us best. We may not have realised it at the time, but we were probably much more magically-creatively-mystically active when we lived by the seashore, in the mountains or woodland, or amongst the rolling

South Downs. Often it is only with the benefit of hindsight that these influences become obvious to us – but *our* individual empathy with the landscape will not necessarily be the same as anyone else's. The view from the Path to the Mysteries will broaden our outlook, but we will always have a stronger link to some locations than others.

In the Glen of Aherlow, for example, the mountains are Old Red Sandstone – a tough enduring rock formed during the Caledonian Foldings, the mountain-building period of the Earth's long history. The pressure caused the underlying softer Silurian rocks to fold into great ridges; and over millions of years the erosion dust compacted to form this magnificent range of Red Sandstone mountains. The Galtees are Ireland's highest inland mountain range, a high ridge which rises up almost sheer from the surrounding plain. Two major Ice Ages have affected the area, and the rounded summits of the Galtees are due to the higher parts being above the ice. This freeze-thaw action on the higher peaks gradually wore them away to form the stony, scree-covered summits we see today. This glacial action also formed cirques (or corries) on the higher slopes – amphitheatres or hollows, which are now five gloomy lakes.

As previously observed in *Magic Crystals, Sacred Stones* and *The Hollow Tree: A Beginner's Guide to the Tarot and Qabalah*, because sandstone is highly susceptible to weathering and decomposition, and ultimately crumbling to dust, we can safely assign it to the Element of Earth. Or more precisely, the 'Earthy part of Earth' symbolised by the Princess of Disks in the Tarot, who represents the 'element of the brink of Transfiguration'. She has been depicted with her sceptre descending into the Earth where the point becomes a diamond, and her shield denoting the 'twin spiral forces of Creation in perfect equilibrium'.

This might go a long way in explaining why, since living in the Glen, this author has produced ten books in quick succession, several of which had been lying dormant for several years. The energies of the Glen are 'dark' – not in any negative sense – but because the primitive history of the place is unchanged and unchanging. And if, like me, you are someone who is attuned to primitive energies, then the magical/creative urges will be stimulated with a vengeance when living in such a magnificent location. The mountains are never the same on consecutive days: the summits are either capped with snow, radiating in the mellow tones of sunset, shimmering in a soft blue haze, cloaked by low-lying clouds and soft rain, or (on rare occasions) crystal clear images of a hot summer day when sheep are seen as tiny pin-pricks of white against the green. And when the river is in high-flood, the Glen turns into a vast lake, just as it was before people came to inhabit this part of Ireland.

The area is truly a ritual landscape, with a passage-tomb on the Slievenamuck Ridge (immediately behind the cottage) that dates to Neolithic times (c.4000–2400BC); with many prehistoric monuments, such as standing stones, surviving in upland areas on the slopes of the Knockmealdown and the Galtee mountain ranges. In the western part of the county there is a dense concentration of barrows, earth-built burial monuments from the Bronze and Iron Ages (c.2400BC–AD400). In legendary terms, Darby's Bed, located, like most Irish passage tombs is on a hilltop site, near the westerly end of Slievenamuck Ridge. A path through the forest leads to this amazing burial ground where one enormous rock slab rests across a number of upright stones.

Before these observations of creative stimulus are dismissed as merely wishful thinking on the part of the writer, I would have to add that I experienced similar literary outpourings when living in my homeland of Wales, near the Preseli Mountains. These hills are also dotted with prehistoric remains, including evidence of Neolithic settlement, and in 1923 the bluestone from the hills was identified with that used to build the inner circle of Stonehenge. Archaeologists have since pinpointed the precise place from where the bluestones were removed in about 2500BC

– a small crag-edged enclosure at one of the highest points of the 1,008ft high Carn Menyn mountain. The stones were then moved 240 miles to the famous site at Salisbury Plain. This discovery came a year after scientists proved that the remains of a 'band of brothers' found near Stonehenge were Welshmen who transported the stones. The skeletons were found by workmen laying a pipe on Boscombe Down and chemical analysis of their teeth revealed they were brought up in South West Wales. Experts believed the family accompanied the stones on their epic journey from the Preseli Mountains to Salisbury Plain.

By contrast, the time between living in Wales and Ireland was spent in the flat, reclaimed lands of Suffolk and rural Leicestershire, and produced hardly anything at all of a truly creative nature. To get any form of inspiration from the latter it was necessary to take a long walk to a spot that proved itself to be particularly strong on magical/creative energies, and that was the granite outcrop at Markfield (Charwood Forest in Leicestershire) that rises up from the Midlands *clay* plain. These rocks are more closely comparable with those of many parts of Wales and represent some of the oldest known anywhere in England. On the western side of this central plain, the magical Malvern Hills are also unlike any other outcrop in England and Wales, and may represent a slice of pre-Cambrian base-rock, which is only found at the surface in north-west Scotland. Weekends spent in the Malverns also produced a surge of creative energy that quickly diminished after returning home on the plain. The Suffolk sojourn produced absolutely nothing at all, to the point of atrophy – although for a close friend who is both pagan and a very talented photographer, the open, flat landscape of East Anglia is a very magical place indeed.

If in any doubt as to recognising the suitability of a particular location, perhaps we should include a pendulum amongst our possessions.

- Try to pinpoint your own *personal* energy spot by using a pendulum that contains an element of quartz. Dowse the site thoroughly and calculate where the energy is the strongest from the pendulum's reaction.
- If a location seems unsuitable for magical or inspirational working, then a short journey might make all the difference. For example: the short distance between the clay plain levels at Charnwood and the granite outcrop was only a short walk away from each other.
- Understanding what lies beneath our feet will enhance our magical and creative ability, especially if we can learn to plug-in to the natural energy of the place.

This meditative interlude should provide an outdoor 'temple site' for regular recharging of the mental, magical and mystical batteries that we will need on our journey. Shinto's reverence for Nature stems from the most ancient and fundamental belief that spirit-beings govern the natural world – **a belief shared by many Old Crafter witches**. These Japanese spirits or deities are known as *kami* and Shinto belief is called 'The Ways of the Gods (or Spirits)'. This belief system was originally intensely local, focussing on the spiritual power inherent in nearby topographical features and on the divine Ancestors of clans and lineages; where places of natural beauty contain the 'essence' of the divine spirit – **a belief shared by many Old Craft witches**.

The Hunter's Spirit Guide
Here, in this ritual landscape by the still waters of our ancestral roots, we also need to reflect on the importance of our power animal on the Path to the Mysteries, since this creature will be our guide between the different planes of existence. It should also be obvious why traditional witches are discouraged from identifying with power animals they are unlikely to encounter in the wild as part of the natural landscape.

Hunting, whether for survival or for sport, goes back to the beginning of time and was probably also one of the first focal points for magico-religious practice for our hunter-gatherer Ancestors. This idea is further endorsed by Stone Age cave paintings that feature man pursuing and interacting with his quarry on an active and shamanic level. The animals depicted in these pre-historic underground chambers were the creatures on which early man depended for his survival, in just the same way as Native Americans and Australians were doing thousands of years later. Not only were these animals a valuable resource, they were also the means by which youth proved its manhood, and thus became the totem creatures of the tribe.

The methods by which these animals were eventually pursued and killed obviously included lengthy and elaborate rituals whereby the spirit of the quarry was honoured, both before and after the kill. When we look at the hundreds of colourful images preserved deep inside the caves at Altamira, Chauvet-Pont-d Arc and Lascaux, for example, we enter the early world of the hunter taking steps to assure the success of the hunt. Archaeological investigations reveal that many of the images at Lascaux had been repainted several times. Most were also so deep inside the caves that the artist would have needed some form of lamp to accomplish the work. These two facts have led academics to suggest that the paintings had important social and/or magical significance, showing that the two earliest forms of mystical observance were connected to burial/death and the hunt.

So, how did this extraordinary art develop? And what purpose did it serve? And how did it happen to survive intact over so many thousands of years?

H W Janson, former Professor of Fine Art at New York University, wrote that the last question can be answered easily enough, 'for the pictures never occur near the mouth of the cave, where they would be open for easy viewing (and destruction) but only in the dark recesses, as far from the entrance as possible.' Some can be reached only by crawling on hands and knees, and the path is so intricate that the visitor would soon be lost without an expert guide. Hidden away as they are – they are located in the bowels of the Earth, to protect them from the casual intruder – these images must have served a purpose far more serious than mere decoration.

There can be little doubt, in fact, that they were produced as part of a magic ritual to ensure a successful hunt. We gather this not only from their secret locations and from the lines meant to represent spears or darts that are often found pointing at the animals, but also from the peculiar, disorderly way the images are superimposed on one another.

For the Old Stone Age people, there appears to be no clear distinction between the image of an animal and the 'reality of its being'. The creation of an animal brought the creature itself within killing range, and the image of the animal's vital spirit was brought down. Therefore a dead image (one on which the killing ritual had been performed) was of no further significance and could be disregarded when it became necessary to renew the spell.

The magic worked, too, we may be sure, since hunters whose courage was thus fortified were bound to be more successful when slaying these formidable beasts with their primitive weapons. Nor has the emotional basis of this kind of magic been lost even today.

Even so, there remains a good deal that puzzles us about the cave paintings. Why do they have to be in such inaccessible places? Couldn't the hunting magic they serve have been performed just as well out in the open? And why are they so marvellously life-like?

Would not the magic have been equally effective if the killing had been practised upon less realistic images?

It has been suggested by Professor Jansen that perhaps we should regard the cave pictures as the final phase of a development that began as simple killing magic at a time when big game was plentiful but shifted in meaning when the animals became scarce (there is evidence that the big herds withdrew northwards as the climate of Central Europe grew warmer). Perhaps the main purpose may no longer have been to achieve the kill but to 'create' animals by increasing their supply, or to make them return to the locality. Were these underground chambers the early 'temples' of the hunter-priesthood, typified by the horned shamanic figures so common in cave art?

Evidence to support this hunter tradition has also been offered by archaeologist Paul Bahn, who points out that another significant factor in the choice of location for images of the hunter's quarry are the acoustic qualities of the caves. Today we tend to enter these caves speaking in hushed tones but, he suggests, this may be wrong; the original artists or users of the caves may well have been singing, chanting or praying loudly while the images were being used or made. 'We will never know, but investigations of acoustics in some Ice Age decorated caves have detected a correlation between the locations of decoration and those places where men's voices can best be heard.'

It is in inescapable fact that magic played a very important part in hunting, and our Ancestors relied for their success as much on supernatural agencies as on natural means, while an unsuccessful hunt was ascribed less to lack of skill or inadequate weapons, than to the failure of some preliminary ritual, or possibly to the stronger magic of some rival force. That is why, even today, there is a very clearly identifiable ritual carried out prior to the start of a hunt when the Master partakes of the traditional stirrup cup before moving off.

Our thoughts about our Ancestors, however, are not about their hunting abilities but on the actual animals they hunted and the relationship that animal had within the tribe. The bear, for example, would have been a formidable adversary for Stone Age man, but in killing the animal the family would have been provided with meat, fat, furs, implements and decorative items – and as such its spirit must be honoured and appeased. The bear would then have become the family (or clan) totem or power animal and given special abilities in interacting with the family's spiritual welfare as a psychopomp. The bear subsequently featuring in their cave art would have become a sacred or protective image for the extended family, tribe or clan.

As Old Craft witches, we will have identified with our own personal power animal a long time ago, and this is the companion that will be journeying with us on our Path to the Mysteries. The power animal, according to the definition given by anthropologist Michael Harner, is conceived as a protective tutelary spirit that helps or guides an individual and acts as a mediator between the unconscious and conscious realms. It is therefore essential for those on a mystical quest to have forged a strong bond with this protector and guide well in advance of the journey – and to have chosen an animal they would expect to encounter in the wild.

The Journey Continues...

It was Marian Green in *A Witch Alone* who observed that 'the path in any study is hard, and that which leads through the hidden worlds of Witchcraft perhaps even more so, because it is dealing with intangible things'. Here we are confronting Jung's unconscious and conscious realms, the multiplicity of archetypes and the overwhelming influence of the past; changes of viewpoint and perspective and the ebb and flow of completely unfamiliar tides.

As *Traditional Witchcraft for the Seashore* observes, it is an overused analogy to say that we are all on a journey of discovery, but it is indisputably an accurate description of how we are all moving towards an inevitable end. Our original journey began in the misty and mysterious fountain that welled up amongst the rocks on the distant mountain slopes of childhood. It passed through the changing landscape of brooks and streams of adolescence, and on through the marshes of our teens before entering the calmer tributaries and rivulets of adulthood; the vast river moving us through our mature years until we reach the estuary and shore of the great sea where our journey ends – and begins again as we retrace our footsteps ... *And know the place for the first time ...*

At this stage of our journey it is a good idea to introduce the reader to the writings of Chet Raymo – that unlucky seeker after the green ray mentioned in Chapter Two. Professor of physics and astronomy, a teacher, naturalist and writer, his work explores the relationships between science, Nature and the humanities, brimming over with mysticism. In *Honey from Stone* and *The Soul of the Night*, he explores the values of the traditional religion of his childhood and asks what value it has in the contemporary scientific cosmos, and whether scientific knowledge is a satisfactory ground for spiritual experience.

Written in the 1980s, in a series of lyrical reflections, the professor explores the wonder of the natural phenomena he sees all around him – the beauty of the fossils he finds along the coast, the brilliance of meteor showers on a nearby mountain. Along with our witch's cord and knife, these two books should be the companions on our journey, together with our power animal and pendulum. We can dip into them at random when we have the need of some spiritually uplifting message, or when we take time for a spot of reflection on our quest. As Raymo observes in *Honey from Stone*, it is not a work of metaphysics or theology – more of a 'serendipitous adventure, a spiritual vagabond's quest' from which '...I took whatever scraps of revelation I could find. I sought the burning bush and did not find it. But I found the honeysuckle and the fuchsia, and I found the gorse and heather. When I called out to the Absolute, I was answered by the wind. If it was God's voice in the wind, then I heard it.'

In his writing Professor Raymo's metaphysical scepticism has great value for the witch in that it forces us to re-examine our own convictions and beliefs. These are *not* magical books, but there is a considerable amount of reflective mysticism to be found in the pages. We will return to him again and again on our quest, but as we leave this world of still water there will be no time for further reflection until we stop beside the woodland pool.

Try This Exercise:

If we take the opportunity to re-examine our own convictions, we must – sooner or later – be forced to ask ourselves the following questions:

- Why do we need Mysteries within witchcraft?
- Why do we feel there are Mysteries to be drawn toward?
- Do such Mysteries really exist?
- Are the Mysteries a myth?

The answer to these questions at this stage of our journey is probably going to be: I don't know! Whatever our convictions or belief, we have no *physical* evidence to prove anything and all that has been written and spoken about the Mysteries since ancient times could be nothing other than a beautiful fiction.

And yet the properly trained, traditional Old Craft witch has an intuitive instinct for the unknown and the unknowable – that 40 percent information and 60 percent intuition that tells us that we don't yet have any of the answers to our questions.

Chapter Five

Crossing the Dark River (Lower Reaches)

Mysteries: Among the ancients, secret religious rights or ceremonies, to which only the initiated were admitted.
[*Ward and Lock's Standard Etymological Dictionary*]

The real breakthrough on the Path to the Mysteries is the witch's ability to view 'God' (or however we view He, She or It) without the trappings of religion. That is to say, accepting the Divine Power, however we choose to feel it manifest, without it being decked out in the persona of a benign or bad-tempered patriarch, an archetypal hunter, a universal mother, or divine child. Not only that, when a large number of contemporary pagans view the concept of belief, the darker elements of Deity are often conveniently overlooked in the process. We need to understand that Deity, irrespective of Path or Tradition, is not there as some kind of divine lottery, handing out bouquets and brickbats.

Again with the absence of genuine pagan 'scripture', we can find similar historical examples within Shintoism, in that there is a belief of a superior or 'divine' realm which informs and guides human existence. The word *kami* is often translated as 'Deity' but in fact it refers to an extremely wide range of spirit-beings together with a host of mysterious and supernatural forces and 'essences'. As C Scott Littleton explains in *Eastern Religions*:

The Shinto tradition does not believe that there is an absolute dichotomy of good and evil. Rather, all phenomena, both animate and inanimate, are thought to possess both 'rough' and 'gentle', or negative and positive characteristics depending on the circumstances.

Depending on the circumstances, every witch experiences at some stage or another, the meaning of 'darkness' – that sensation of utter loneliness and despair that periodically engulfs us in a blanket of doubt and resentment. We have no doubts about our magical ability, or about the Path we've chosen to tread, but suddenly a strange, suffocating malaise settles over us and we're powerless to disperse it. Like the lower reaches of the river, the gulf is deep and wide, with the current deceptively sluggish. The flow of the water deposits silt on the bends cut out of the banks during the winter flooding – and this is what is happening to us at this stage of our journey. We've become mentally and emotionally bogged down in silt and sluggish water through being pulled in too many directions at once. In the lower reaches of the river there is an almost soporific atmosphere amid the weeping willows, reeds and water lilies.

Instead of coming out of our reflective thoughts at the still water stage in a revitalised frame of mind, we are plunged deeper into despair and uncertainty. This is because we have plumbed the depths of our soul and realised that this journey is for real; we are in a state of mourning for the past and uncertainty about the future. This mental sensation of mourning brings about the recognised stages associated with physical bereavement: shock, numbness, loneliness, anger, disbelief and even guilt, not to mention the over-riding sense of loss and unreality. These are sensations brought about by the death of the past as Frances Wilkes explains in *Intelligent Emotions*:

In order to come to terms with these losses we mourn them until we're ready to let them go. Grief is the doorway from one state to another and it is essential for change and development. Grief doesn't feel very comfortable but it's exactly this discomfort that's needed to force us to move on ... The goal of grief is to achieve an integration at a higher level than we were before we lost the thing we mourn.

When we talk about the 'dark night of the soul' on a mystical level, we are grieving for those things we have left behind, and for the loneliness of the Path ahead. We may feel guilty for abandoning our fellow witches; or anger because they refused to share our vision. Whatever we feel at this stage of our mystical quest it won't be long before we alter our opinion of how we view our beliefs and the Old Craft teachings for good or ill.

The concept of God/Deity as creator/destroyer is an extremely ancient one and those of us on a mystical quest will quickly begin to realise that there isn't an omnipotent controlling power that can be appeased by mere prayer or offering. The bad things that happen in life are not dictated by the whim of a malevolent Super-Being, although the other form of 'darkness' is, of course, the concept of evil that is undoubtedly one of the most ticklish of all theological questions. Is there really any such thing as the personification of evil? Perhaps the best answer is one from the Qabalah:

> Evil is simply misplaced force. It can be misplaced in time: like the violence that is acceptable in war, in unacceptable in peace. It can be misplaced in space: like a burning coal on the rug rather than the fireplace. Or it can be misplaced in proportion: like an excess of love can make us overly senti-mental, or a lack of love can make us cruel and destructive. It is in things such as these that evil lies, not in a personal Devil who acts as an Adversary.
> Dion Fortune, *The Mystical Qabalah*

Questions such as these demand answers and sometimes the answer we receive only makes us even more insecure or frightened than ever. The more information we gain when we're following the Path to the Mysteries just goes to prove how small and insignificant we really are in the universal scheme of things. We suddenly start to question our reasons for starting out on this ridiculous journey in the first place. Why couldn't we have stayed at home, safe and snug instead of negotiating threatening river currents and clambering up treacherous mountain slopes in search of enlightenment!

For the moment the best thing a witch can do is go with the flow and see where the currents of the lower reaches of the river will take us.

Going With the Flow

Going with the flow encourages us to view these misgivings and uncertainty with a certain degree of calm as the currents of the river may lead us to some *kensho*-type experiences. If we allow the current to carry us along, we may find ourselves encountering still backwaters, wide flowing basins, white water rapids, and even the Styx or Lethe, to use a mystical reference. This mysterious river, however, isn't all smooth sailing, but travels within the confines of its banks even when running at flood tide; should it break out from those naturally confining barriers, it becomes unmanageable and dangerous.

When we allow the current to carry us along, however, we may discover other mysterious places we didn't know existed, or look at the view from a different perspective – but if we have no control over our craft, we can be swept back out to sea instead of continuing up river. The more we allow this process to inspire our thoughts, the more adept we become of knowing when to throw out the anchor; in the meantime we let the inspiration of the moment carry us where it wants us to go. As long as we keep the banks in sight, we can always steer ourselves back to shore and continue our journey.

The world of the witch is a strange one at the best of times. Most of our Old Craft experience will have been going about our normal lives observing the natural cycle of the Wheel of the Year. As *Traditional Witchcraft for Fields and Hedgerows* points out, the magical energies for the fields and hedgerows that lie either side of the river are of a much more domestic and homely variety. This is the comfy zone of witchcraft – in meadowlands running down to the river and high hedgerows where we find a treasure house of food, drink, medicine and fuel that provide the fundamentals of our Craft. We often need to return to these basic skills to get grounded when we encounter the dark night of the soul, but it is during this dark time that our eyes begin to see. And this, writes Chet Raymo in *The Soul of the Night*, is the paradox: that black is white, that darkness is the mother of beauty, that extinction of light is a revelation...

> Perhaps it is only in the dark times that the eye and the mind, turning to each other, can cooperate in the delicate and impassioned art of seeing. Few people willingly choose to walk the dark path, to enter the dark wood, to feel the knot of fear in the stomach, or to live in the black cave of the sleepless night. But then, unexpectedly the truth emerges. The light of the mind returns bearing extraordinary gifts.

This is where the witch finally grasps those magical and immortal words of William Blake and understands that we really *can* see a world in a grain of sand and heaven in a flower. That it *is* possible to hold infinity in the palm of our hand and live eternity in an hour. On the other hand, it is just as well that the colours of the stars are not easily seen. As naturalist John Burroughs observed, if the deep night were revealed to us in all its naked grandeur, it would perhaps be more than we could bear – like looking at the face of God – however we perceive it to be. 'But half of infinity is still infinity too – if we can take the hint. A trait here, trait there. Of hints and traits we make our way.'

The Journey Continues...

The lower reaches of the river have also provided suitable sites for settlement since the earliest part of our history when the people changed from hunter-gathers to agricultural settlers. We still remain within the safe confines of our familiar world; our minds and emotions may be moving on, but our physical body is reluctant to let go of the bank and start swimming *against* the current of convention. The familiar world we've known appears to be slipping away from us – or we from it. The traditional witch still feels the need for security of the roots from which we draw our succour, but in our heart of hearts we know it is time to move on regardless of the consequences.

It was Transcendentalist Ralph Waldo Emerson, the friend, mentor and fellow of multi-talented Henry David Thoreau, who observed: 'He who knows what sweets and virtues are in the ground, the water, the plants, the heavens, and how to come to these enchantments, is the rich and royal man.' We must now go out and discover these 'sweets and virtues' for ourselves and as the scales fall from our eyes, we find that we can observe the world around us with delight and wonder, but without the mawkish sentimentality that often accompanies such pagan musings.

The lower reaches of the river is also a place of more change in that our journey will become less urban and more rural. Although we will not be moving far from the allegorical riverbank, the river itself will be slipping away from the world of people – the urbanised river bank of dog walkers and Sunday afternoon strollers – for we are about to enter the world of the Great God Pan.

Try This Exercise:

The witch's backpack is easy to carry since we have jettisoned all the glittering baubles, fancy robes and magical equipment in favour of travelling light. We wear the pendulum on its cord around our neck and our witch's girdle around our waist; the knife is carried in its sheath on our belt and the power animal runs free ahead. The only things we carry in our backpack are copies of *The Soul of the Night* and *Honey from Stone*, which are now our personal scriptures for the purpose of aiding meditation.

On a mundane level begin sorting through your personal magical regalia and see what can be discarded. Of course, there will be many items that have sentimental value, but much of what we have in drawers and cupboards we will have outgrown and can be disposed of sensibly. Divide these belongings into three separate boxes:

- Items that you wish to retain for personal use (including magical books) should be carefully packed and stored away until you are ready to look at them again. Put them somewhere safe in a cupboard or loft away from prying fingers and eyes.
- Items (including books) that you would like to pass on to friends or fellow witches can be handed over as they are – it will be up to the recipient whether they cleanse them or choose to retain the essence of your magical aura in the gift.
- Items that can be donated to charity shops should be thoroughly cleansed before leaving the house. Beginners' books that we've kept at the back of the bookshelf for years should be added to this box.

We are making a statement to ourselves that a certain part of our Craft life is over and that we are taking a physical step in clearing out the magical clutter from our environment. There will be certain items that we really can't part with for a variety of reasons, but this is the opportunity to get rid of any

superfluous possessions. We all love to work with beautiful objects as part of our Circle workings – and there is nothing wrong in this – but for the time being these should also be put away until we are ready to use them again.

Chapter Six

Pursuit of the Absolute (Woodland Pool)

Mysticism: The doctrine that man may by self-surrender and spiritual apprehension attain to direct communication with and absorption in God, or that truth may be apprehended by the soul without the intervention of the senses or intellect.
[*The Waverley Modern English Dictionary*]

A witch's mystical quest does not demand that we jettison belief as a whole just because we now see things from a much wider perspective, since it will eventually lead us towards the more mystical aspects of our own faith, whatever we perceive it to be. Here we should recall the subtle differences between the *kensho* and the *satori* experiences – and how they can also apply to Old Craft mysticism.

For example: many things happen on the periphery of our 'vision' – occurrences that are so fleeting that it is only with hindsight, or when someone else talks about a similar experience that we remember them. Under normal circumstances the lack of an acceptable explanation or interpretation discourages us from exploring further even if it leaves a residue of puzzlement in our mind. Those on a mystical quest may find that these 'gateways between the worlds' or different levels of consciousness, make them more aware of the open channel between these strange experiences.

Once developed, the mystical side to our nature enables us to interact with life on a cosmic scale, not merely confining ourselves to the mundane world. We may feel that this appears to smack of grandiose platitudes, but it is what is meant by the now outdated terms 'microcosm' and 'macrocosm' – illustrating the tendency of humankind to picture both Deity and landscape in his own image. The Universe is regarded as a human organism on a gigantic scale and mankind as a miniature copy. Although esoteric thinkers of the Renaissance adopted the theory, it was well-known in medieval Europe, which in turn had inherited it from the Classical world, where the Universe was considered a living and divine organism. Currently no longer regarded as having any scientific value, the theory has retained immense significance for present-day esoteric thinking; satisfying two powerful opposite feelings that mankind has about itself and its place in the universal scheme of things. These ideas are also illustrated by the mystical Qabalah, reflecting the relationship between humanity and the Universe, while encouraging correspondences between the differing forces in the Universe and their equivalent in man.

This is demonstrated within traditional British Old Craft where the *intellectual* concept of Pan as the 'Horned God' (rather than the stag-antlered Cernunnos), has become firmly entrenched albeit flavoured with a Renaissance acceptance of Pan Pangenator, the All-Begetter, who transcends all limitations – he is All. He is also The Piper at the Gates of Dawn depicted in *The Wind in the Willows,* and the unnamed terror that introduces 'panic' into the sensations of the Wild Hunt. Or as Dion Fortune described it in *The Winged Bull*: 'Panic is what he produces in the unprepared, but in whose who are prepared for his coming he produces a divine inebriation' – the natural, chemically induced endorphin rush that heralds the sensation of 'the lifting of oneself into a wider consciousness'.

> The gods of men's worship were not things in themselves, but the creations of the created – the forms under which man represented to himself his ineffable Creator and Sustainer, the form changing as man's power of understanding increased. The forms did not matter ... You could help yourself to the kind of god that suited you, so long as you realised that he

was only a dramatisation. The real thing was behind all the gods, and no man had ever dramatised It. On your head be it if you made yourself a nasty god who liked blood-sacrifices; or a silly god who wanted to make a pink sugar confectioner's heaven of this tough old earth. The nearer you got to the facts in your conception of God, the better for you, but no man's concept had ever been the truth, the whole truth, and nothing but the truth, nor ever would be. When he reached that stage he would just quietly pass out and go free. God was the Absolute, whatever that might mean.

Dion Fortune, *The Winged Bull*

The Absolute is commonly referred to as the One and we are all an essential part of the One. This means that our inner-most self is identical with the Absolute with its unchanging power against a backdrop of the changing Universe. This also means that we do not live solely within our own lives, but within the life of the Universe, which has its foundation in a changeless being; which is at the same time one's own eternity. Therefore, although the seeker is aware of the One behind the many faces of Deity, we can still feel ourselves to be an integral part of that Oneness. This is simply because all things come together in the One just as spokes form a bridge between the rim and the hub of a wheel – and the wheel is a universal symbol of spiritual harmony – the first being cosmic consciousness. The second is the realisation of eternity and the true implications of the state of 'deathlessness' – that the 'soul' cannot die. The third is the union of the soul with the Absolute in much the same way as a Buddhist's belief in Nivarna.

Needless to say, none of this philosophising would have been applicable to the mind-set of an Old Craft witch of the 1800s, but it made perfect sense to the emancipated witch of the mid-1900s, who was beginning to stretch the esoteric boundaries of learning. But for all this pushing and 'expanding' of the intellect, traditional witchcraft still recognised – as Swinburne and Nietzsche recognised – that the old Gods were not without significance and that mankind had lost a lot by neglecting them. And as Dion Fortune observed: 'By reawakening them we recover the use of the subconscious mind, and we get in touch with great natural forces from which civilisation has cut us off.'

The energy that emanates from the woodland pool has none of the tranquillity of the still water we've left behind because we've taken the first step in passing out of the realms of stifling civilisation. It is here amongst the trees of our native landscape, by the woodland pool, that we reawaken those 'great natural forces'. As this author observed in *Traditional Witchcraft for Woods and Forests*, if the fields and hedgerows are often considered to be the province of the Goddess, then the woods and forests are certainly the realm of the Horned God, since first and foremost, forests and woodland have played a mystical role in all cultures where trees have dominated the landscape. Trees bring Nature right up close and personal and, as a result, the whole of the natural world becomes a tangled web of enchantment to a true witch's eyes.

In reality Old Craft does lean towards the male aspect of Deity since the female remains veiled and a mystery. In other words, the 'God' is the public face of traditional British Old Craft while the 'Goddess' remains in the shadows, revered and shielded by her protector. Not because she is some shy and defenceless creature, but because face to face she would be too terrible to look upon! Nevertheless, it is amongst the trees of ancient woodland that we come face to face with the Old One, or in some cases, are pursued by Him. Who has not experienced the presence of the God when walking alone in the woods and suddenly feeling that we are being hunted, or that rushing feet are coming up behind up, only to turn and confront – nothing? Except for the unearthly sound of laughter fading in the undergrowth.

Although not generally acknowledged, there are areas of the forest known as the Wild Wood that are dark and untamed, where unearthly and potentially dangerous beings are still to be found. This is not always welcoming and many urban witches never get over an atavistic fear of Nature uncontrolled. On a magical level, the Wild Wood refers to those strange, eerie places that remain the realm of the Horned God and untamed by man.

Ancient gnarled oaks, festooned with ferns and draped with lichen, carry an air of solitude and remoteness that is deeply unnerving – here birdsong and the trickle of the stream are the only sounds to break the silence. It is the realm of Pan and the Wild Hunt. Here among the trees, we are never sure whether what we see is reality or illusion.

Nature's Mirror

The symbolism of the woodland pool is often lost on those who come across them in small clearings in the dense undergrowth. Often these pools are transient things that disappear and re-appear at the whim of the seasons; more often than not these shallow depressions are choked with fallen and decaying leaves that create a dank, stagnant pond. And yet there *is* a sense of Otherworldliness about the still, dark depths of a pool that lurks in the shadow of the trees like Galadriel's mirror – waiting for us to look into it to know the past, the present and the future.

For all its gloomy appearance, in winter the woodland pool spreads out around the roots of the willows, where an invisible hand creates slow ripples on the surface of the water to suggest the illusion of timelessness. Although some of our forests are ancient, nothing remains from the prehistoric days except for 'traceries in rock and a few plant parts preserved by quirks of geology'. According to author of *Forest*, Jake Page: 'This fossil record, supplemented by informed conjecture, has enabled scientists to reconstruct many of the key plants that lived 370 to 345 million years ago.' And yet there are subtle links with this ancient past if only we know where to look...

These primitive trees, flourishing long before the first animals appeared on the land, resembled their present-day counterparts only in the barest outline; the conifers and flowering trees of today would not evolve for tens of millions of years. Instead, nature had improvised this dawn forest from some of the humblest of plants: enormous relatives of the spore-bearing, moisture-loving club mosses, ferns and horsetails that carpet low, shady spots on the floor of modern forests.

These are insignificant plants that we overlook when walking through the forest, but they provide a direct link with our mystical past and we should respect them accordingly. Belonging to the *Pteridophytes* classification, ferns, horsetails and club-mosses are vascular plants (composed of vessels conveying liquid) that have leaves known as 'fronds', roots and sometimes true stems; they do not have seeds or flowers and reproduce via spores – as they have done for 300 million years and provide another example of Blake's musing on seeing 'heaven in a flower'. Here by the dark woodland pool we can find these humble plants that link us with the primordial world via the advances of modern palaeobotany (from the Greek words *paleon* = old and 'botany', study of plants): the study of fossilised plant remains.

Scrying in these natural surroundings is usually spontaneous and often produces quite alarming sensations, but the woodland pool is Nature's Mirror and who could resist the urge to take a peek? The dark water makes the perfect scrying tool in the shadow cast by the overhanging branches. This method comes under the general heading of hydromancy although there is a vast difference in interpreting the signs from the comfort of a homey bowl of water and the raw, naked energy of the woodland pool. The signs may appear in the form of patterns on the surface of the water, shapes dimly perceived in the inky blackness of the pool, or ripples made from drops of water or rain.

Although one of the oldest forms of divination, scrying is

simply achieved via meditation while staring at the play of light on the reflective surface of the water. After a period of quiet meditation, ask your question – either aloud or silently – while staring into the water; the answer is received clairvoyantly or in a misty message in the depths of the pool. There may be a sense of being watched, or even a hardly discernible shape looking up from the bottom of the pool.

The woodland mirror should not be used for trite questioning or in a spirit of mockery – or you may find yourself on the receiving end of some sylvan mischief that you weren't expecting!

The Journey Continues...

The woods and forests are the buffer-zone between the past and the present, and for most witches they are places of sanctuary and tranquillity away from the mundane world. There among the trees is a place of mystery and enchantment and so much of this has left its own footprint on our legends, myths and folklore. As the 1928 classic *The Lore of the Forest* tells us:

To a wanderer in forest solitudes a sense of mystery is often perceived which lures him on and on into the verdant depths of the woodland world. On a brilliant summer day the tremulous throbbing of the air, seemingly full of whisperings and sighings from an unseen host, appears like the pulsation from the mighty heart of the forest, while, all around, sunlight and shadow form a tangled web of enchantment, which is deepened by soft elusive perfume floating on damp zephyrs. In fancy he may feel drawn back to the early primitive ages, when the forest deities would have had a very real existence to him, and he would understand the inner meaning of those oracles which were often spoken in the glades of the primeval woods.

This magic extends through every season of the year from the shimmering spring beauty of the beech woods; the lush tree canopy and cool shadows of summer; the rich tapestry of autumn to the winter when trees glimmer with hoarfrost. 'It has been said that the forest knows all and is able to teach all; that the forest which always listens, has the secret of every mystery.' And in *The Catalpa Bow: A Study of Shamanistic Practices in Japan* we find that trees, particularly tall pine trees, are often considered the dwelling place of *kami* (spirits).

But it is now time to leave this temple of Nature to follow the meandering river that snakes its way through the landscape in a series of serpentine shapes ...

Try This Exercise:

If we truly wish to experience the 'Presence' we should try the following call taken from Aleister Crowley's *Hymn to Pan*, which has been used by all and sundry for years, simply because it works:

IO PAN! IO PAN!
IO PAN! PAN! PAN!
IO PAN! IO PAN!
IO PAN! PAN! PAN!

This should be repeated over and over again when walking in the woods, timing each word to the rhythm of your step. Remember that the word 'panic' comes from Pan, so be prepared for an over-whelming sensation of fear. Nevertheless, the exercise can produce some very intense moments of Horned God energy!

Be warned: Do not call upon the Great God Pan unless you are prepared to encounter Him face to face when alone in the depths of the woods.

Chapter Seven

Faith in Doubt (Meander)

Mystic: Those who profess to receive, in holy contemplation, true religious knowledge, or impressions directly from the Divine Spirit. [Ward and Lock's Standard Etymological Dictionary]

'I consider it a sign of human weakness,' wrote the Roman natural historian Gaius Plinius Secundus, 'to inquire into the figure and form of God. For whatever God be, and wherever he exists, he is all sense, all sight, all hearing, all life, all mind, and all within himself.' While Pliny's song to the Earth is one of the most beautiful passages in his *Natural History*: 'She receives us at our birth, nourishes when we are born, and ever afterwards supports us; lastly, embracing us in her bosom when we are rejected by the rest of nature, then she covers us with a special tenderness.'

Continuing our own analogy of the journey along the river, Pliny continues: 'The water passes into showers, is concreted into hail, swells rivers, is precipitated into torrents; the air is condensed into clouds, rages in squalls; but the earth, kind mild, and indulgent as she is, always ministers to the wants of mortals.'

As any witch knows, however, the Earth cannot withstand the power of Water – and Water, the prime Element of our journey demonstrates this in the form of a river's meander, a distinctive serpentine river feature caused by the movement of silt from the uplands. Some of this will be deposited wherever an obstruction occurs, and the river will curve as its flow is diverted from one bank to the other. As the position of the meander gradually moves downstream the channel curves from side to side, creating a flat valley floor and slowing the river even more. With the continuing process of erosion the curves in the river channel develop into broad loops called meanders, while the current cuts into the outer side of each bend, forming sheer banks. The time scale for this can be calculated by comparing old maps of the county boundaries (which often followed the old course of the river) with a current one.

The question of how and why rivers meander has intrigued researchers for a long time since a large number of factors can cause a river to change direction. In *Rivers and Lakes*, Laurence Pringle explains that it may be turned aside by an erosion-resistant rock formation or by a chance obstacle, such as a large boulder of a fallen tree. 'But such random happenings can hardly account for the striking symmetry of meander bends, or for the remarkable similarity of bends in streams of different sizes in diverse physical settings.' One widely held theory was the Coriolis force, which is exerted by the spinning of the Earth upon its axis, but modern research suggests that this force is not suffi-cient to bend all those rivers and that the meander is merely a naturally occurring energy-saving mechanism caused as the river adjusts to the variations in its depth, velocity and slope.

Meanders commonly occur where a river traverses a gentle slope that is covered with fine-grained sediment; as the stream enters a curve, centrifugal force hurls the faster-moving water near the surface against the outside bank of the bend, eroding it in the process.

> The fate of the sediment eroded from the outside bank is determined by the peculiar hydrodynamics of meandering. While the surface water hugs the outside bank, the slower water nearer the bed compensates for this, tending to move toward the inside bank ... As a result most of the silt picked up from the outer bank is deposited on the inner bank of the next curve.

As we make our mystical journey inland from the sea, witches are always conscious that although the force of the water erodes the land in one place, at another point it begins to create a new landscape. In lowland rivers, whirlpools are often found to be caused by the meandering of the channel causing erosion on one bank with corresponding deposits on the opposite bank. In meanders that are particular sharp and which have eroded a deep pool in the stream bed, the whirlpool is at its most powerful, for the full force of the water is driven into a sheer, often crumbling bank that turns the water full circle.

In mystical terms the meander's sinuous, serpentine symbolism is reminiscent of the maze or labyrinth, often at the heart of Old Craft teaching, where to 'tell the maze' is an important element. In colloquial English, the word 'labyrinth' is generally synonymous with 'maze', but there is a distinct difference between the two. A maze is a complex branching passage through which the seeker must find a route. In everyday speech, both maze and labyrinth denote a complex and confusing series of pathways, but technically the maze is distinguished from the labyrinth, as the labyrinth has a single through-route with twists and turns but without branches or dead-ends, and is not designed to be as difficult to navigate. A traditional witch will understand the significance of these different aspects and discover the wonder of the analogy within the natural landscape.

Historically, magically and symbolically, the Cretan labyrinth is the oldest, and in Greek mythology it was an elaborate structure designed and built to hold the Minotaur, a mythical creature that was half man and half bull; in Minoan myth the Minotaur was known as Asterion, meaning 'starry' or 'ruler of the stars', which offers a completely different explanation of the symbolism of what we find at the centre of the labyrinth. 'Minotaur' is simply a Hellenic description of an iconic bull-man image; but coins minted at Knossos from the 5th century depicts a kneeling bull or the head of a Goddess crowned with a wreath of corn, while the reverse shows 'four meander patterns joined at the centre windmill fashion, sometimes with sickle moons, or with a star-rosette at the centre' [Karl Kerenyi. *The Gods of the Greeks*]. The Romans created decorative labyrinth designs on walls and floors in tile or mosaic; those on the ground being large enough that the path can be walked in both group ritual and for private meditation.

The full flowering of the medieval labyrinth came about during the 12th-14th centuries with the grand pavement labyrinths of the Gothic cathedrals – the one at Chartres being the most famous. Vincent Sablon, writing his *Histoire de l'auguste et vénérable église de Chartres* in 1671, attributed the original site of worship to the Druids, but there is no evidence for this – except for the strange mystical ambiance created by the master masons with their sacred geometry – held by some to represent the lost knowledge of the builders of the Temple of Solomon and the Order of the Knights Templar.

> The floor at Chartres is not checkered or patterned or tiles. It is made of slabs of limestone ... But as we become accustomed to the light in the cathedral we perceive that the floor itself is reflecting the colours from the glass, changing with the time of day. The general effect is olive and purple with here and there spots of bright colour from the newer glass. John James compares this vast area of tawny stones to a billowy sea, for as the diffused sunlight changes, 'the paving seems to heave and swell, its bumps and irregularities expand like the texture of the sea' ... Only when the doors are locked ... The halls lie muted. Only light and pattern remain – quiet and undemanding'.'
>
> *Chartres: The Making of a Miracle*, Colin Ward.

Set in this huge, rough-hewn floor is the labyrinth: 12 metres in diameter, the meandering path of white stones, separated by thinner blue ones is 294 metres long. Entering the cathedral by the main door, the small entrance to the labyrinth is immediately ahead, which architect Keith Critchlow described as an image of the cosmos, suggesting that 'the body of the cathedral reflects a reconciliation between Lunar and Solar cycles and the psycho-logical forces of which they are the physical embodiment'. There are two other interesting points of note: 'the great twelve-fold west rose window not only conforms basically in size to the maze, but when hinged down onto the floor of the nave covers it almost exactly'. Secondly, there was once a copper plaque in the centre bearing the images of three figures: Theseus, the Minotaur and Ariadne – three pagan figures in the heart of a Christian shrine.

And if we associated the symbolism of the meander to the labyrinth, we can also associate the whirlpools often found in this part of the watercourse with the spirals that decorate the Megalithic and Neolithic monuments we will encounter as we begin our climb upwards from the valley floor. Possibly the most stunning examples can be found at Newgrange, in Ireland, a passage-tomb constructed around 3200BC – which makes it 600 years older that the Pyramids at Giza and 1,000 years older than Stonehenge. At the Winter Solstice the light of the rising sun enters the roof-box, penetrates the passage and shines on the floor of the inner chamber for just 17 minutes. Originally the shaft of sunlight would probably have illuminated the famous triple spiral on an inside wall.

The spiral has one uninterrupted path sweeping inwards to the centre and can be found in every type of setting from remote mountainsides to lowland tombs and solitary megaliths. From the Iron Age, however, the use gradually diminished and the religious symbolism was lost – just like the spiritual elements of the labyrinth at Chartres in a much later age.

Nevertheless, the spiral remains the oldest design that links today's witch with our remote Ancestors and as we work our way along the river, the occasional, naturally occurring whirlpool echoes the spiral on another level of consciousness.

The Path of the Mystic

It is when we reach this stage of our journey that our meditation and contemplation pays dividends and we receive the true knowledge of belief, or impressions directly from the Divine Spirit. Or what Aleister Crowley describes as 'conversation with the Holy Guardian Angel' – and, hopefully, know that we have arrived, or are about to arrive, at the Gateway to the Path of the Mysteries.

Hopefully, we have also discovered what Shintoism defines as *wa*, or 'benign harmony', which should be inherent in both Nature and the human condition; anything that disrupts this state is considered disruptive to the achieving of inner peace and therefore bad. *Wa* echoes the state of *ma'at* of ancient Egypt, in that if *wa/ma'at* is disrupted then everything descends into chaos. Anything that contributes to *wa* is, by definition, good; those things that disrupt it are perceived as being fundamentally evil. 'This belief also applies to humankind's relationship with Nature and underscores the pervasive Shinto concern with maintaining a balance between the human and natural realms,' C Scott Littleton explains.

Once we have passed through the Gateway it is almost as though an invisible portcullis has slammed down behind us, cutting off our retreat. There can be no turning back and now that it is too late, we fully understand what Crowley meant when he wrote about oath breaking:

The candidate is pledged quiet simply to himself only, and his obligation binds him merely to 'obtain the scientific knowledge of the nature and powers of my own being'. There is no penalty attached to the breach of this resolution; yet just as this resolution is in contrast with the oaths of other orders in respect of simplicity and naturalness, so also with regard to penalties…

The oaths taken within any Tradition should be deemed to be sacred and, because in the esoteric world the punishment always fits the crime, it is inadvisable to betray that Tradition or any individual fellow member without expecting some kick-back. When a member takes an oath, whether it is made publicly or privately, it is to him or herself, as well as to the Old Craft, and involves making certain statements on, or by, the Power in which we believe. Anyone joining anything of their own free will be required to take some form of oath or vow by pledging themselves to conform with the 'regulations' and subsequently, in breaking them we blaspheme only ourselves.

In other words, in breaking our oath, we are betraying *ourselves*; we are no longer fit to walk the Path of the Mysteries and must suffer the consequences of our actions. The penalty we incur is reflected in the old adage of 'what goes around, comes around', in that we will eventually 'reap what we sow' and will be 'paid back in our own coin'. Unfortunately this kind of metaphysical justice gathers momentum as it travels in spirals around the astral plane and revisits the oath-breaker with all the velocity of catching the 'down express in the small of the back' to parody Wodehouse.

All witches need to be aware of these repercussions and not take the breaking of an oath lightly. You will have brought it upon yourself, and will only have yourself to blame.

The Journey Continues…

The meander is a spectacular creation – from the gentle, sinuous curves of the English meadowlands to the gigantic sweeping curves of the Archafalaya River in Louisiana before it empties into a bay adjoining the Gulf of Mexico. Symbolically our mystical journey follows the path of the watercourse just as the true path through the labyrinth has a single through-route with twists and turns but without branches or dead-ends, and is not designed to be as difficult to navigate as the maze with its hidden complexity.

As the slope of the valley levels out and the curves in the river channel develop into broad loops, the valley widens into a broad plain with the stream snaking back and forth across its down-valley axis. Our mystical journey carries us along this meandering course so that we are constantly revisiting familiar vistas but always viewing them from a slightly different viewpoint.

Like all pathways, however, our mystical journey will not always be smooth sailing. Although the flow of the meander is slowed down considerably by its twists and turns, there are always hidden trials and tribulations to hamper our quest. If the flow of the water is increased due to heavy rain or melting snow then our gentle river can still become a raging torrent, flooding its banks and creating swirling currents as it encounters rocks or other obstacles. Even during the calm, there will always be the swirling whirlpool, produced by the meeting of opposing currents and where obstructions are found that divert the water into a narrow channel, whirlpools are usually found immediately downstream.

In Shinto belief, one of the most common symbols is the *mitsu-tomoe*, a triple comma-shape that also has the connotation of a swirl, or circular motion, sometimes depicted as an eddy or whirlpool. These three commas linked together as a circular symbol represent the 'visible' manifestations of the soul: its creative, calm and turbulent aspects, while the spaces between signify that which is hidden, mysterious and abstract in the Universe, marking the place where the different aspects of the soul (or the Universe) interact and overlap. 'This circle represents perpetual motion, the constant cycles of life, death and renewal that govern all aspects of the Universe, including divine forces,' explains Aidan Rankin in *Shinto: A Celebration of Life*.

Looking back along the Path we've trodden so far, we begin to realise just how wide and varied the obstacles are that separate us from our goal, and we are still in the lowlands. We haven't yet started the long, hazardous climb to the summit of our mountain. What we have achieved, is the recognition of those sacred signs and symbols that will act as guides and messengers to keep our feet firmly on the Path and our eyes on our ultimate goal. Our witchcraft has metamorphosed from a humble personal ability into a full-blown mystical quest.

Try This Exercise:

In Shinto belief, a rock formation, a freezing waterfall, a snow-capped mountain, a forest or even an ordinary looking tree can be points of connection with divine power or the spirit world. As Aidan Rankin reminds us, 'the original Shinto was highly local, but it was also universal – an aspect of primal spirituality that saw nature as the gateway to something higher than oneself and reminded humanity to live as if nature mattered.' At this stage of your quest can you feel that you are:

- An integral part of the planet?
- An integral part of the universe?
- An integral part of creation?

Such flashes of insight are not as rare as people would like to believe. Although the experiences are fleeting the seeker harbours no doubt of the reality of the sensation. We are being introduced to totally new and different forms of consciousness, which we will find almost impossible to describe to those who have not shared a similar experience. Do your best to make a record in your mystical journal.

Chapter Eight

The Power and the Glory (Lowland Lake)

Mysteries: In Greece, secret forms of worship, involving religious doctrines revealed only to the initiated, and probably connected to beyond the tomb.
[*The Oxford Companion to Classical Literature*]

Unlike rivers, which are long-lasting features of the landscape, lakes are ephemeral, observed Laurence Pringle in *Rivers and Lakes*. Rivers endure; they serve as drains that remove wastes; their waters, always in a state of youthful renewal, carve new channels, ensuring survival. Lakes grow old; they serve as sinks that collect wastes; imprisoned in their own basins, they gradually fill up with sediment and become dry land.

Mirroring a similar gradual obsolescence, Professor Steve Jones, author of *The Descent of Men*, observed that all men, towards the end of the last millennium, must have felt a sudden tightening of the bowels with the news that their services as progenitors had been dispensed with since cloning was now a scientific reality. From a magical perspective, a systematic form of emasculation has been going on for some years to such a degree, that in many forms of modern paganism, what we refer to as 'the old Horned God energies' have almost been eradicated in favour of Goddess-worship

During the past 30 years, the role of the male in modern witch-craft has changed out of all recognition. Those watching from the sidelines have witnessed how distanced Wicca has become from the Path of the Old Religion, with its contemporary preclusive Goddess-worship. Males have found their ritual role diminishing to the point of being nothing but a cipher in modern practice – although traditionally the chalice had always represented the female principle and the knife, the male, to symbolise balance. On a ritual level many may say that these changes are for the better, but for genuine magical practitioners, this is not the case. Within Old Craft both parties have equal input, with the male and female working as a complete and well-balanced partnership to enhance the flow of positive and negative energy depending on the nature of the rite and the type of energy to be raised.

The various permutations required for raising and maintaining this magical equilibrium is surely a significant factor in regard to the role of the priest and priestess of any Path or Tradition.

It is not just within Craft circles, however, that this imbalance is occurring; it is spreading through the entire social system, and even through Nature itself. Unfortunately it has gathered such a head of steam that it has tipped the scales in completely the opposite direction and men have allowed it to happen as if there was some need to atone for the centuries of exploitation and suppression of women. From the magical and mystical point of view it is imperative that the male role within witchcraft is restored, otherwise all forms of genuine traditional Craft will disappear completely.

Perhaps this can be explained in less emotive terms in that many Shinto practitioners use Yin-Yang imagery, based on the Daoist concept of two polarities or complementary principles, such as hot and cold, hard and soft, masculine and feminine, light and dark, positive and negative, active and passive, mountain and valley, Heaven and Earth. Yang represents the harder, and at the same time more abstract energy, associated with mountains, Heavenly power and pure intellect; Yin represents the softer, more Earth-centred energy, associated with valleys, subtle powers and intuition.

Each of these principles, crucially, contains an element of the other and together they make up the whole. Neither makes sense or is complete on its own. An overemphasis on one (at the expense of the other) produces imbalances, whether physical and psychological within individuals, or social and political within the larger human community. *Yin and Yang are not hostile poles, but complements that continuously and creatively interact.* So it is with the magical and mystical elements of witchcraft.

Putting the Y-Chromosome Back into Magic

What really divides the Craft community is the basic lack of understanding about operational magic and mysticism *per se*, and if people choose to ignore these elements of witchcraft then why are they following, or claiming to follow, a belief that is based on the interaction of these dual energies and which requires paying more than just lip-service to the Horned God? Today, the Horned God has been all but excluded from modern pagan practice and this is often a result of the feminist development, where the majority of groups often appear to have problems relating to an all-powerful male Deity.

In Nature, the Goddess is symbolically ravished, brutalised, abandoned and, once the harvest is over, left to shrivel and rot. The God is the instrument of her death, even though he watches over her while she sleeps through the long months of winter.

The role of the Sacrificial God has a much wider significance, in that his death is brought about for the collective good of his people. In magical terms, to eradicate the protective male/God aspects would be tantamount to the complete annihilation of the Old Ways because we approach the Goddess *through* him. An Old Craft witch does *not* summon the Goddess because she is perpetually hidden from us, like the dark side of the moon. We know she is there, and occasionally we may be aware of her presence, but it is not a face that anyone would willingly want to behold! In this way, the Horned God is our protector, too. Needless to say, this fearsome, darkened image of the Goddess figure is not the one used within popular pagan imagery.

To truly understand the dual-gender of the Mystery Tradition, however, we need to step back into the Ancient World to appreciate the subtle nuances of the different experiences. Basically the female Mysteries are related to Death and Rebirth; while the male Mysteries are geared more towards Death and Resurrection. A subtle difference and there are, of course, overlapping elements between the two aspects but to tread the Path of the Mysteries requires an understanding on both sides that the male role is every bit as important as its female counterpart. In various aspects of magic it may mean that the male needs to take the active role while his partner remains passive; in other types of rite the female is the activator while the male remains passive. This is because male energy and female energy whilst compatible are essentially different – just like their genetic make-up. Just as the preparation for the Mysteries follows a similar Path – the eventual outcome will be dissimilar for those of a different gender.

Generally speaking, formal Initiation into the Mysteries comes about following a series of rites and oral teachings whose purpose, according to that eminent anthropologist Mircea Eliade, is to produce a decisive alteration in the community status of the person to be Initiated. 'In philosophical terms, Initiation [into the Mysteries] is equivalent to a basic change in existential condition; the novice emerges from his ordeal endowed with a totally different being from that which he possessed before his Initiation; he has become another.'

Through a long period of training the seeker gains access to the traditional knowledge of Old Craft, undergoing a series of ordeals along the way. And it is primarily these ordeals that constitute the mystical experience of Initiation – the encounter with the sacred. As Professor Eliade explains:

The majority of initiatory ordeals more or less clearly imply a ritual death followed by resurrection or a new birth. The central moment of every initiation is represented by the ceremony symbolising the death of the novice and his return to the fellowship of the living. But he returns to life a new man, assuming another mode of being.

Initiatory death signifies the end of innocence, ignorance, and the profane condition. All the rites of rebirth or resurrection indicate that the seeker has attained another level of existence, inaccessible to those who have not undergone the same ordeals, those who have not 'tasted' death.

There were certain male and female Mystery Traditions that were extant in historical times – the Mithraic and Eleusinian Mysteries, the rites of Dionysus, Orpheus, Isis and Osiris – that were highly complex and whose importance in the religious and cultural history of the Eastern Mediterranean was considerable. All were founded on divine myth, with which the participants were already familiar – the descent into the nether world and the dismemberment of the God prior to rebirth and resurrection when the seeker became one with the Gods. *'I know thee, Hermes, and thou knowest me: I am thou and thou art I.'* Or as Professor Eliade wrote:

Though abstaining from revealing the secrets of the various Hellenistic mysteries, many philosophers and theosophists propounded allegorical interpretations of the initiatory rites. The majority of these interpretations referred the rites of the mysteries to the successive stages through which the human soul must pass in its ascent to God. Any acquaintance with Iamblichus, Proclus, Synesius, Olympiodorus, as of many other Neoplatonists or theosophists of the last centuries of antiquity, suffices to show how completely the assimilated the mystery initiations to a psychodrama through which the soul can free itself from matter, attain regeneration, and take its flight to its true home, the intelligible world. In making this assimilation these writers were continuing a process of spiritual revaluation that had already found expression in the mysteries of Eleusis.

Understanding Hermetic philosophy will not enable us to crack the code of these ancient Mysteries but it serves to show that *both* the male and female Mystery Traditions were of considerable importance in antiquity. Also that many of the rites were similar in essence if not actuality with the shamanic customs of other more 'primitive' societies into which traditional British Old Craft falls.

We can also see from the predominantly male Mithraic Mysteries that the ancient deities that we recognise as the Elements, no longer confined themselves to heaven, according to Dr Franz Cumont, author of *The Mysteries of Mithra*. 'Their energy filled the world, and they were the active principles of its transformations.' Fire was the most exalted: revered in all its manifestations, whether shining in the stars, or in bursts of lightning, whether it animated flora and fauna, or lay dormant in the bowels of the Earth. 'In the deep recesses of the subterranean crypts it burned perpetually on the altars, and it votaries were fearful to contaminate its purity by sacrilegious contact.'

This ancient priesthood also had the same superstitious respect for the saline water of the oceans, 'the springs that gurgled from the recesses of the earth, the rivers that flowed on its surface, and the placid lakes resplendent in their limpid sheen. A perpetual spring bubbled in the vicinity of the temples, and was the recipient of the homage and offerings of its visitors.' The Earth, the nourishing mother, held just as an important place in the doctrine if not the rituals of this ancient belief; while the four cardinal winds [Air] were looked upon as manifestations of the deified seasons, were invoked as spirits to be loved and feared.

Feared because they were the capricious arbiters of the temperature, which brought heat or cold, tempests or calms, which alternately moistened and dried the atmosphere, which produced the vegetation and withered the foliage of autumn, – and loved as the diverse manifestations of the air itself, which is the principle of all life. In other words, the doctrine of the Mithraic Mysteries deified the four simple bodies which, according to the physics of the ancients, composed the universe.

In *Adam's Curse,* geneticist Professor Bryan Sykes turned his attention to the only piece of DNA that men possess and women do not – the Y-chromosome. In scientific surveys this has been linked to aggression, but despite the increased rise in violent crime and the continuing conflict around the world, far from being vigorous and robust, this traditional genetic symbol of maleness is decaying at such a furious rate that men are in danger of dying out! It is not as simple as the idea that the female holds all the material that will sustain reproduction and that the male merely has some material to be harvested and stored. What has been eroding maleness with oestrogen since the 1970s when the Pill became every woman's right in the Western world, are the billions of gallons of flushing lavatories in the West which have contaminated the water supplies – and are also altering the male-female ratio in other species on the planet.

The idea was originally mooted that the aggression-related attributes of male testosterone is something that would be better eliminated from 21st century society, but in doing so the magico-mystical balance would also be destroyed. For our primitive Ancestors and the defenders of their tribe or clan, we accept that with violent predators to fight off, hominid males had to be strong and powerful. Needless to say, this desire to protect one's own home and family is now contrary to the law and the man who resorts to violence in order to protect what belongs to him – be it be his mate, his children, or his home – is likely to find himself in court as a result.

Any Old Craft witch will retort, however, that such an enfeebled or emasculated specimen is of no Earthly (or Heavenly) use to the 'Goddess', since he would be totally useless as either progenitor or protector. When we refer to the archetypal repre-sentations of the God in the Wild, in his capacity of Consort, we are celebrating the power of the male on a much higher and deeper level than mere sexual beings. The Horned God and the Goddess are creatures of the Wild, and do not sit comfortably in homespun or scented drawing rooms with dilapidated males dancing attendance on females who have become much more selfish and assertive; who only have concern for others if they are female, and exclude males from the equality stakes.

In today's society it is the norm to equate all male roaring and pouncing, or aggressiveness with violent or threatening behaviour, rather than the strong male need for the physical challenge of pitting their strength or endurance against daunting obstacles such as mountains, seas, jungles or deserts. In fact, some armchair pundits decree that such activities should be banned because of the danger. Magically speaking, the Y-chromosome is a vital ingredient for well-balanced working relationships, and it takes real courage to follow the Wild Hunt, or undergo the ordeal of Initiation into the Male Mysteries.

All magical and mystical working has an element of danger and it would be unwise to claim otherwise; just as only the uninformed would dismiss the need for both male *and* female input into traditional British Old Craft.

The Journey Continues...

For a witch, the lowland lake is an ideal metaphor for the Mysteries in that on the surface they are 'resplendent in their limpid sheen' with the sparkle of sunlight on the ripples in the water. Here is peace and beauty. We can marvel at the magnifi-cence of the rich tapestry of trees and plants in the water margin; the reflection of the mountains casting a reverse image on the surface of the lake. And yet beneath the surface there is another world of light and shadow, of deep and shallows, of death and decay, which represents the reverse side of Old Craft teaching.

The river feeding it has flowed some miles from the distant mountains and the water here is deep and slow; the current is no longer strong enough to move boulders, but the water carries particles of mud and sand towards the outflow at the other end of the lake. The margins fringing the lake grow wider, and so does the valley with the land sloping gently towards the water. Most lowland lakes have muddy bottoms and are surrounded by soil (rather than by rock), consequently the margins are rich with varied and colourful plant life.

Lakes have been formed in a variety of ways, but the most common were once plains that lay under a sheet of ice that brought with it soil and boulders scraped from the land as it advanced. When the ice melted it left behind hollows that filled with water, forming shallow lowland lakes that still exist today. This contrasts with other areas where the ice, concentrated by narrow valleys, gouged long, deep and narrow trenches. Others have been form by damming, subsidence or, as in the case of the Norfolk Broads in England, human excavation – digging for peat in medieval times.

Universally, lowland lakes are shrouded in myths and legends, often synonymous with traditional witchcraft, such as the mystical Llyn y Fan Fach near the Black Mountain in Wales; the Arthurian Lady of the Lake who is associated with several lakes in the British Isles; while all across the world the native people have a rich and varied folklore concerning their local lake. This watery realm has been handed down in both folktale and legend as a powerful and persistent strand of Otherworld belief.

The concept of a world of power beneath the water, which has been transmitted through oral tradition is also a remarkably constant one in Shinto belief – just as it was for the indigenous peoples of the British Isles.

Try This Exercise:

The lowland lake offers a witch the wonderful opportunity for meditation and divination. This is often the place where our Ancestors saw the entrance to Otherworld and all manner of unearthly beings were thought to lurk in its depth. The waters of the lake can be just as treacherous as the open sea despite its land-locked location, so do not be deceived by the tranquillity and beauty of the place – like all things magical and mystical, the lake contains elements of both darkness and light.

Before embarking on the pathworking, make an offering to the spirit of the lake in the form of a 'precious' object such as a silver coin. Find a spot where you can stare down into the shallows without there being a danger of falling in. Here we should find small fish hovering in shoals close to the bank and on these we focus our attention and visualise ourselves slipping into the greenish water to join them. As we descend into the cool water we are conscious of the bright sunlight above, filtering down through the rippling depths. We imagine ourselves hovering in the gentle current, but this is no time to relax because somewhere in the gloom lurks a predator – the pike.

Pike usually stay close to the bank where weeds are dense, but they may stray into deeper water in a large lake. This fish has been referred to as the Water-wolf, the Lord of the Stream, the Freshwater Shark, the King of the Lake – and a large number of anglers consider the appellation well deserved. In some ways the pike is more savage and ruthless than the shark and is a formidable opponent, and to catch one calls for skill of a high order, and in country lore there is hardly a deep water hole in any part of the country that does not house a pike of astounding dimensions. Even when the pike has been landed, it can still be a handful and, hours after it has been caught, can inflict severe wounds on the unwary.

As we hover in the water we see the large head and gaping mouth of this monster – *but this is what we've come to find*. A worthy power animal with whom we can empathise since a witch learns from an early age how to lurk in the shadows, unseen and unmoving; and there are times when we may need to be as ruthless and savage as this 'Water-wolf'. A witch needs to be just as difficult to corner and be able to inflict injury on an enemy that would attack us. We need to make a split decision ... do we flee or do we tread water and ask our question of this terrible hunter?

This pathworking takes a lot of courage to follow through even though we know that we are enacting it on a psychic level, this is the first time we have intentionally put ourselves at risk. Although there is no physical danger the success of the pathworking is reliant on our confronting this perceived threat and emerging triumphant from the water of the lake.

Chapter Nine

River of Consciousness (Upper Reaches)

Mysteria: Involving closer contact with divinity. These began as agrarian rites, then acquired the initiatory aspect and soteriological functions, promising a blissful afterlife.
[The Penguin Dictionary of Religions]

The practice of traditional British Old Craft often consists of the understanding of magical opposites, and if the beautiful lowland lake was often considered to be the entry to Otherworld, the upper reaches of the river is the perfect analogy for the magical adage 'As Above, So Below' in that here we also find the awesome world of the underground river. What thriller writer John Connolly, author of *The Killing Kind*, describes as a honeycomb world that hides a hollow heart, while introducing Democritus' famous saying: 'That the truth of nature lieth hid in certain deep mines and caves;' we are led further into these underground arteries of mystery and wonder ...

> The stability of what is seen and felt beneath our feet is an illusion, for this life is not what it seems. Below the surface, there are cracks and fissures and pockets of stale, trapped air; stalagmites and helactites and unmapped dark rivers that flow ever downward. It is a place of caverns and stone water-falls, a labyrinth of crystal tumors and frozen columns where history becomes future, and then becomes now. For in total blackness, time has no meaning.

But before plunging into the Stygian gloom of Connolly's 'honeycomb world' we need to meditate on the wonders of the upper reaches of the river. To help us find inspiration in our surroundings, we can reflect on the fact that Shinto shrines are often erected in these inaccessible spots of breath-taking beauty. As in this Japanese Nature poem for example:

Among the hills
The snow still lies –
But the willows
Where the torrents rush together
Are in full bud.

In *The Great Religions by Which Men Live*, by Tynette Hill, the chapter 'Shinto: The Way of the Gods' tells us that a follower of this Path:

...sees himself as only part of the living, inspiriting wonder of everything that exists. He has a feeling of nearness to nature that the average European or American does not have. The Japanese have always felt the lure of the outdoor spaces – the sand, the wind, the stars, the waves, the hum of the insects, the music of a waterfall. The Japanese believe that the same wonderful forces that move in nature move in themselves.

E'en in a single leaf of a tree
Or a tender blade of grass,
The awe-inspiring Deity
Manifests itself.

As always, this simple animistic belief gives us a workable, clear-cut template for what modern Western paganism professes to be about, before it became over complicated with borrowed tenets and philosophies in an attempt to fully explain itself to the successive generations. For Old Craft, simplicity remains the key-word – in other words there is no dividing line between the human and the divine in that life and belief 'have entered into each other so that it is almost impossible to tell where one begins and the other ends'.

The upper course of the river is characterised by a steep descent and the inflow of many small tributaries; it is usually narrow and fast-flowing, eroding a distinctive v-shaped channel that zigzags between interlocking rocky spurs. The rate of flow along the upper course may be highly variable, depending on seasonal factors such as snow-melt or heavy rainfall, and most mountain rivers are subject to regular flooding even at this high level.

It is here, along the upper course that we begin to notice the difference in atmosphere as the actual physical pathway begins to get steeper. The surrounding landscape becomes more rugged, often cold, bleak and windswept – but surprisingly rich in both flora and fauna. In *The High Kingdom*, Robert Gibbons observes that surprisingly these uplands are among the most artificial of all habitats because, although almost all the land up to the natural tree-line (which can be as high as 2,000ft) *should* be wooded, hardly any of it exists now. This bleakness is entirely man-made because the uplands have changed dramatically during their long history.

From being stripped totally bare by the last Ice Age (some 10,000 years ago); through a long period of dense forestation; to the present time where the uplands are open grass and moorland that have been systematically closely cropped by sheep. Most of the native wildlife failed to adapt to these changes and the fauna that lived in that dense wooded area have now gone – yet eagles, ravens, harriers, hares, foxes and other open-country creatures remain. For the witch, who has one of these creatures as a power-animal, will soon discover that its energy becomes stronger in this wind-swept terrain where natural instincts come to the fore; we find that these natural instincts transmit from power animal to human with consummate ease.

These lower mountain slopes are spectacular in their own

beauty, and here and there we can catch glimpses of what the original woodland cover must have been like. The upland river flows over a rocky bed, carved deep into the landscape, sometimes flanked by stunted downy birch and that most magical of trees, the rowan – or mountain ash. Although a popular decorative tree in suburban gardens, the rowan is more usually associated with the high country. In the British Isles rowan grows at altitudes up to 3,115ft, which is higher than any other native broadleaved tree, and, as another close associate of witchcraft, it is comforting to find this 'familiar' at such a wind-swept stage of our journey.

Although the uplands are generally inhospitable, there *is* an enhanced mystical sense of purpose to our journey. As Chet Raymo reminds us in *Honey from Stone*, history leaves its imprint upon a physical landscape; it also leaves an indelible impression upon the landscape of our souls. The Old Craft witch being ever tuned-in to the 'sense of place' is now conscious of walking in a more hostile environment than at any stage between leaving the seashore and arriving at the lowland lake. This is an alien landscape that makes us feel vulnerable and alone but conversely we accept it with the realisation that having come this far, we *are* well and truly on the Path. We have endured and although the going isn't going to get any easier as we climb higher into the mountain, the ultimate goal is worth the sacrifice and danger. This is the experience for which nothing prepares us because we are conscious that whatever it is that we have undergone, the sensations will have been different for those who have instructed us – and different again for those who follow in our footsteps. Our *kensho* experience is unique and we share it with no one else!

Every river seeks out the smoothest gradient and straightest possible route to the sea, and the upper course of the river is also characterised by picturesque waterfalls and rapids. Rapids form where a river rapidly cuts downwards through the rock along its bed, where uneven rates of erosion leave large rocks standing above the tumbling white water. The power of a river is seldom more clearly visible than in and around waterfalls; often occurring when the geology of the riverbed changes from a hard rock to a relatively soft one; at the base of most waterfalls the waters erode a plunge pool, which is gradually enlarged by the scouring action of rock fragments from the cliff-face.

For the Japanese shaman the acquisition of power is via the trial of cold water. 'To stand under a waterfall, preferably between the hours of two and three in the morning and preferably during the period of the Great Cold in midwinter is believed to be an infallible method of gaining power,' writes Carmen Blacker in *The Catalpa Bow*. Sacred writings reveal that during the medieval period the Nachi waterfall at Kumano was considered a powerful means of accumulating power. As Blacker continues: 'This celebrated waterfall is now, especially after heavy rain, of such weight and force that to stand beneath it is a scarcely credible feat.'

Pilgrims on the way to a sacred shrine will also undergo this cold water exercise as a means of cleansing to rid 'oneself of defilements repugnant to the *kami*'. Clarity and concentration of mind are said to be the virtues frequently cited as resulting from the cold water and whilst the force of the water on a bare head is stunning even from the most modest trickle, the exercise has been known to bring on pneumonia! The banks of the upland river are littered with large boulders that have been eroded higher upstream and carried down in times of flood, gradually being reduced in size by abrasion as they rub against each other and against gravel on the river bed. Since we still have a long way to travel, we will have to be content with sitting on one of the boulders and ritually washing our hands in the icy water of the upland river in a gesture of reverence.

As groundwater from the rain seeps downwards through the limestone, tiny fractures gradually enlarge into the open passages of John Connolly's 'honeycomb world'. When upland streams and rivers are swallowed by these caves, erosion continues more rapidly. Underground rivers scour out huge waterfall shafts, and dissolve great tunnels through the limestone; those above the water-table, cut deep, twisting canyon passages, by the removal of limestone in solution and sediment abrasion of their floors. Below the water table, caves are full of slowly moving water that dissolves limestone walls, floors and ceilings. Many of these passageways descend steeply to the water table and then flow sideways as flooded passages until they intersect the surface where the emerging water flows toward a natural outlet that feeds the surface upland river. As the river gradually erodes the valley floor, the water table drops and the water in the main underground channel seeks new paths to this lower level. While young, active caves have noisy streams and cascades, old abandoned caves are silent wonderlands decorated with stalagmites and stalactites, which we will encounter along the last stages of our journey.

As a result of these experiences, the witch will always be conscious of the underground waterways that flow beneath our feet – representing the stream of unconsciousness on a psychic level.

The Journey Continues...

During our time in this bleak, rocky wilderness we come to realise that if history leaves its imprint upon the physical landscape, as Chet Raymo observes, it *really* does leave an indelible impression upon the landscape of our souls. This is also a perilous place to be. Here we find ourselves encountering the scree slopes – banks of loose, bare stones where living things can at any moment be buried by rockfalls. Typically the stones of a scree slope are sharp and angular, not rounded like those worn by water and found on the beach.

As Robert Gibbons describes for us in *The High Kingdom*, many mountainsides exposed to weathering have broken into vertical cliffs whose loosened fragments are scattered down the slopes by the force of gravity. 'They are common in upland districts and contribute greatly to the wilderness of the landscape.' This is one of the few surviving locations left relatively undisturbed by man and can be considered along with mountain cliffs and corrie lakes as an almost natural – and therefore precious – element in the mountain scene.

Although we are climbing the lower reaches of the mountain, we suddenly discover that the ground beneath our feet isn't solid as we'd expected – the scree slope is like a running, upland river of loose rock that can sweep us away at any moment. And many of our long-held beliefs and concepts are in danger of being swept away, too. Here, in the 'High Kingdom' we breathe in the pure air of knowledge as various students studying with the Coven of the Scales have discovered as they journey towards the end of their induction course. As former soldier and Desert Storm veteran, C, observed:

I think I'm slowly turning a corner that makes me want to ask if I'm limiting myself unnecessarily? Specifically, I have operated on the principle that, as a [Old Craft] witch, my power(s) are contingent on the favor of a deity. What is coming to me lately is the idea of a Universe outside of what I know as 'Myself' – as 'Other'. So, can I just interact with/command/work-magic-upon this Other without *asking* for favor? I think I understand that 'It' will respond to command; I don't have to deify it or ask it. This is what it feels like is happening. It seems as though the lessons act on one level, but there is something else going on at a deeper level.

This student had picked up on the fact that while an Old Craft witch respects the deities he (or she) should not be reliant upon them for the success of his magical/mystical workings. At the end of her course K performed the obligatory Vigil and observed the following:

> I had a profound awareness that I am but a little, a smallest part of the Universe and being part of that wholeness brings the awareness home in one's self in a profound way. I do feel the spiritual side of my Craft has been lacking focus, I've been more of a 'practical get things done' crafter and not working on myself, since I tend to be very reactionary and can go off at a tangent, which I needed to bring into balance. Now I have a sense of the 'All', call it the Divine; something bigger encompassing the whole of the Universe and it's within me and I am part of it. There is now a new awaking, just like a snake sheds its old skin and I've shed mine as well as my out dated mindset. I feel I want to honour that vastness that I can only begin to imagine, which I felt was as old as the hills. I have felt this before briefly but it soon faded and I trod the maze again. Now I know I want to dedicate myself to this 'force', which I can only refer to now as Oneness with that primal energy that breathed life into all being. To be a vessel for this energy to manifest, to seek balance and harmony, to temper the energies within and become a more whole and rounded person, with mercy and severity when needed, but being aware of the bigger aspect of it all. I can honestly say that during these last few weeks I have felt an inner stillness, a more balanced feeling within myself, a kind of shift since the Vigil.

On a more advanced level, a highly experienced member of Coven of the Scales described the results of a guided meditation. Perhaps the results were produced because North is always regarded in esoteric terms as the 'Place of Power', but this came through as extremely powerful imagery:

The first wind that seemed to capture my attention was the North Wind. Before me stretched a vast expanse of dark space lit by the cold blue/white twinkling of the stellar bodies. The scene was cold and void and I loved every aspect of it, because I knew that somewhere out there was a mighty power waiting to be called and welcomed back to these realms. Between the archaic galaxies, a chill wind started to blow towards the circle and me. Its icy sharpness cut the surface of the skin like a thousand minute fine needle-points. There was a sensation of knowledge and enormous power, but also of destruction, darkness, fear and chaos. It was as if the Great Old Ones who created humanity had decided to return and see how their work was progressing. I experienced a total lack of sentiment, as we usually know it, and in its place was a feeling of the end of all time when false forms are cast off and you stand face to face with eternity. Perhaps when death itself has died.

Slowly I tried to channel the North Wind down from its lofty regions to the Earth plane, and gain mundane knowledge of it. The home of this wind on Earth is the high snowy mountain passes, or the tumbled chaos of the icefields of the Arctic or Antarctic. When working with this wind I was intolerant to people and noise, and longed for the freedom and solitude of those isolated places. I was reminded of the peoples of the Andes and Tibet as well as the Eskimos. My parting experience of this wind was that it was a wind of freedom and transformation that offered much to those who were committed to learning and service to magic. To me a good title for this wind is the Elder Wind because it brings change.

This type of meditation is not, of course, without its risks and should not be undertaken merely for the thrill of the experience. And yet, like the other two examples, it is just

another small step towards making that 'giant leap for mankind' in terms of a mystical quest.

Try This Exercise:

Here at the side of the upper reaches of the river, choose the phase of the moon when your *personal* magical energy is at its strongest. Check on the time of moon-rise, and unless you are going to work on the dark phase, you should try to ensure that the moon is visible throughout your pathworking. For this first, simple exercise we are going to bathe in moonlight and let its rejuvenating powers wash over us, and because this is a very individual exercise there are no instructions other than to go with the flow. For all moon phases, sit in the moonbeams, watch them as they glow all over and around you like shimmering silvery mercury. You can pick handfuls up and watch them stream through your fingers like fine sand or silvery water.

- How does that make you feel?

If you are using the dark phase, simply gaze up into the dark sky above, and allow yourself to drift out into the comforting darkness; visualise yourself slipping deeper and deeper into the void. There is no danger here and you can return whenever you wish. Let yourself drift out into the softness, where it feels like sinking into beautiful velvet or the softness of unseen feathers. It is gentle, soft and welcoming.

- How do you feel in this black, silent world?

Chapter Ten

Restating Identity (Upland Lake)

Mysterious: Containing mystery; having an air of mystery;
obscure; secret; incomprehensible.
[*Chambers Concise Dictionary*]

If there's one place that an Old Craft witch is going to feel a
frisson of fear and trepidation, it's standing at the barren edge of
an upland lake. This really is an alien landscape, devoid of any
visible flora and animal life because nothing can survive in this
bleak wilderness. The surface of this expanse of water is dark
and ruffled by the cutting wind that blows across the face of the
mountain; there is no escaping from the wind-chill and even
though the sun is shining, there is no welcoming shelter to be
found on the sheer cliff face.

Most of Britain's upland lakes are glacial in origin, resulting
from the great sheets of ice during successive Ice Ages gouging
out deep hollows that eventually filled with water. Normally
these upland lakes are too deep, over most of their area, to
permit light to penetrate and encourage plantlife to grow. Lakes
in the region of hard rock, which provide few nutrients, receive
poor supplies of these essential minerals into the water, which is
lacking in both plant and animal life; the bottom of these lakes
usually remains barren and stony and often any fish introduced
into them eventually become stunted or malformed.

The depths of an upland lake *is* a cold, dark, alien world and,
according to leading authority, G Evelyn Hutchinson of Yale
University, 'none of the other mechanisms of lake creation – not
even earthquakes – can match the slow but enormously powerful
creep of glaciers.' The process of glacial erosion accounts for a
high percentage of lake formation 'and is responsible for more

lakes than all the other geological processes combined'. The majority of these glacier-made basins are less than 25,000 years old, dating from the most recent Ice Age, when immense ice sheets advanced over much of the upper latitudes of the Northern Hemisphere, bulldozing everything in their path.

These effects have only become visible after the ice receded and are known as cirques, a name derived from the French for 'circle' – referring to their distinctive rounded shape when viewed from above. Cirques, corries and cwms are basin-shaped hollows on the steep sides of mountains. These often spectacular landforms are also known by their Scottish name, *corries*, and by their Welsh name, *cwm*; when they become filled with water, the resulting lakes are known as tarns. Some of these hollows were already part of the existing landscape while others were eroded by small glaciers as they moved down the mountainside to the valley below. Lakes of this type reach their greatest depths along the edge closest to the summit of the mountain. It is not surprising that these primitive lakes have a mystical quality all of their own since they have been created by an unstoppable force of Nature, and some of the lakes carved out by old glaciers may be so deep that their bottoms are below modern sea level.

This is where for the flicker of an instant we encounter an 'Other' Otherworld where things are not always as they seem. It is the world of illusion, the reverse side of the 'Tree' ... in fact we have found ourselves in that place of blind alleyways with conflicting directions and deliberately misleading instructions; following the darkened maze, through endless sloping corridors to a distorted hall of mirrors. We are here on the barren slopes of existence suddenly realising that for all our witchcraft we know *nothing*.

The 'Real' Psychic Vampire

As deep and fathomless as the uplands lake is the creature all experienced magical practitioners recognise as the 'real' psychic vampire. As paganism continues to attract more and more people to its ranks, the greater the number of manifestations of psychic vampirism; and generally the advice on how to combat their unsavoury attentions is both sound and effective.

The genuine, natural psychic vampire, however, is not so easily dealt with and in the long-term can be extremely dangerous if not treated, producing symptoms in its victim not unlike ME. Unlike the charlatans that hover on the periphery of occultism, this particular breed of psychic vampire's mind isn't on control – it's on survival. Neither does it need to create the impression that it is powerful because it already has highly developed magical powers. Its charisma lies in the fact that it is generous with its magical 'favours', and is often surrounded by a band of aspiring magical practitioners, all working at different levels.

Although still magically and intellectually a force to be reckoned with, the natural psychic vampire is usually in physical decline – due either to advancing age or illness.

The nurtured group of students provide it with all the energy it needs for survival and while feeding is spread liberally across the group, the occasional bouts of feeling tired and lethargic for no apparent reason are attributed to the normal stresses and strains of modern living, or to an intense bout of magical activity.

This vampire gives its all: teaching magical methods that turn other instructors pale. Under its tutelage the student progresses at a remarkable rate and, within a very short period of time is offered access to the bottomless cauldron of knowledge from which the student is welcome to drink his or her fill. The group is encouraged to meet and work together, either at the home of the natural vampire or as part of a working party that generates a considerable table of psychic energy off which the vampire can feed undetected and without anyone being any the wiser.

The problems arise when the students begin to drop out, or if the ranks of the group is suddenly depleted for any number of reasons; the few who are left are leeched off more and more frequently until there is a systematic burn-out at a dangerously high level. This personal account comes from the former *Comhairle* magazine:

> I was young, eager and found myself in a position of having access to the sort of magical training that just wasn't there for the asking. I was elect. I was also lunch, supper and breakfast. My tutor constantly fed me knowledge and I, in turn provided the psychic energy needed to fuel the ageing vampire's body. Fortunately, being a natural magician I was able to replenish my reserves with little difficulty but having that high level of psychic voltage running through my brain, something had to give. Having been required to cut down on magical working due to temporary domestic and career reasons, I wasn't producing a fraction of the psychic energy previously generated. This did not suit my tutor who was desperate for a regular feeding source and my own health began noticeably to suffer. A mutual magical acquaintance realised what was happening and the problem was dealt with by a series of magically-charged rites and all ties were severed with the vampire – but not without concentrated mental and magical effort. The moral of the story, however, is not so simple and clear-cut. Despite the fact that my health (physically and mentally) suffered, the magical knowledge I received during that time was unprecedented and never to be repeated. It was the price I had to pay and even with the benefit of hindsight, I don't regret it for a moment since what I was given was priceless in terms of magical knowledge and instruction into the Mysteries.

These reminiscences emphasise just how dangerous the Path and participation in the Mysteries can be, and is certainly not for the faint hearted since we may emerge at the other end mad, dead or enlightened. This level of witchcraft is dark and ancient; it draws on energy that we never knew existed and should never be encouraged unless we have received the appropriate training and Understanding.

Like a soldier preparing for battle, it *is* permissible to feel fear since this hones mental alertness and sharpens the senses; but abject terror (or over confidence) can present a danger to yourself and others – and you could be coming home in a body-bag!

The Journey Continues...

Many parts of our mountains and uplands are bleak, cold and windswept, but it is at this point we accept the fact that we have passed through the Gateway and are now well and truly on the Path proper, where we are encountering the primal forces of Nature face to face. Here we are completely alone in a mystical wilderness and there are no books or advisors to instruct us on how to behave. This is what our quest has prepared us for – the ability to draw on our faith in the power of the witch to sustain us for the remainder of our journey.

Traditional Witchcraft and the Pagan Revival helped us jettison the illusions of ignorance, i.e. that because something is old it is not necessarily magical, sacred or holy, and recognise the signposts that are often pointing us in a different direction. The landscape is often littered with natural phenomena that were previous ascribed to our Ancestors; we now know, for example, that many of these 'fairy hills' and 'burial mounds' are a result of geological progress, not man-made creations.

Our fairy hills are drumlins: long, low mounds that were formed from boulder clay and deposited by a glacier. They seldom occur in isolation – generally forming in large clusters known as 'swarms', which often suggested burial mounds to the incoming population. Formed during the last Ice Age, drumlins are still a clear feature of the landscape despite 10,000 years' erosion and played an important part in our folklore.

A tor is a weathered mass of rock that usually stands on top of a hill, thus giving it the legend of being some form of man-made monument. They are of great interest because of their spectacular appearance, and because they provide information about the geological conditions that must have prevailed when they were originally formed by the softer components wearing away; leaving behind the harder material in either vertical or horizontal formations.

The romantic in us would still like to believe that here be dragons, fairies, buried chieftains, or such like, but the more scientific elements of our teaching forces us to accept that *these* particular landmarks are not ancestral monuments – but small testaments to the power and force of Nature. As such they can still represent a power-place, but for the traditional witch it is a power-place of Nature, rather than ancestral in origin.

Try This Exercise:

For this meditation exercise we need to find a location that reflects the natural erosion of the landscape – something like a tor, limestone pavement, drumlin or escarpment that can be found all across the country. If we can gain access to an upland lake, then so much the better. Erosion – the natural denuding action of weathering, water, ice, wind, etc., – is what is happening to us on the inner plane where all the old obsolete concepts and ideas are being eaten away as our inner Self emerges from its dormant stage.

Many of these locations remain much as they were when our ancient Ancestors passed this way; we are looking at the same landscape but through new eyes. We all have our favourite forms of meditation but the ultimate goal is always the same – focussing the mind in order to reach a higher level of awareness and inner calm. In this remote location, our thoughts focus on the natural phenomenon we see before us and when we close our eyes, the image remains in our mind's eye. We have already travelled a long way on our journey and there may be all manner of questions to which you seek answers. During the peace and tranquillity of your pre-state meditation ask the most important question, and then clear your mind of all other thoughts – make your mind a blank and see what results ...

We are susceptible to a sense of place and the sight of a scene of outstanding natural beauty can be extremely moving, but bare, barren landscapes often have their own particular form of rugged grandeur. A witch should see beauty in every aspect of Nature.

Chapter Eleven

Reflections in a Watery Mirror
(Mountain Stream)

Mystery Cult: Devotion to god or goddess, in which secret rituals and doctrine have a place. Initiation often involved purification, instruction and a revelation of the god, usually in sacred drama.
[*The Penguin Dictionary of Religions*]

Witchcraft, in its most simplified form, always retains its strong links with Nature and as anthropologist Christopher Tilley observes: 'There is an art of moving in the landscape, a right way (socially constrained) to move around in it and approach places and monuments. Part of the sense of place is the action of approaching it from the 'right' (socially prescribed) direction.' The method of approach is governed by a combination of place and time – both seasonal and social – while the 'art' is the simultaneous practice of meditation and ritualized operation. 'Flashes of memory, so to speak, illuminate the occasion.' This is part of an Old Craft witch's instinctive grasp of how to behave within a particular landscape, and to recognize the type of magical energy to be encountered there.

Even here on the mountainside, equally as important is adeptness in identifying the location of Nature sprites or 'numen' – the spirit-essence dwelling in each natural object: a tree, a spring, a rock, or more correctly, where the presence of Deity is suspected but undetermined. Although numen are usually considered to be an 'essence of Deity' rather than Deity itself, the Old Craft witch treats them with the utmost reverence and respect.

The usual concept of such spirits is of neutral powers that might be hostile if neglected, similar to those of ancient Rome, which if duly placated with offerings will be friendly and give health and prosperity. As a result, any site that inspired status on account of its own magical power, became sacred because it was 'the dwelling of a spirit, or had been touched by its power'. These sentiments were also expressed by the poet Ovid [*Fasti*, iii, 263 and 295]: '*There is a lake, girt with the dark wood of the valley of Aricia, sanctified by an ancient feeling of awe* ...' and '*There was a grove below the Aventine dark with the shade of holm-oaks, and when you saw it, you might say 'there is a spirit there'* ...'. This was, however, a cult of individual natural objects, but was in no sense a worship of the powers of nature.

A Nature sprite is the kind often encountered as the guardian of an individual rock or stream. They can also be guardians of animals and of specific natural landscape features, but these spirits are bound to one particular place. There are certain places where it is easier to contact them, usually where mankind has not intruded too much into the landscape, or where the land has been largely left to look after itself. These spirits have individual personalities and it is possible to create an understanding either with an individual or with a specific 'family' of Nature sprites. Although long-lived, their lifespan is often connected to a part of the landscape; should this be destroyed, then the nature-sprite will die.

There are, however, different kinds of Nature sprites that are often referred to as 'elementals'. Some are the naturally occurring kind usually linked to specific natural features e.g. cliffs, ponds, lakes or mountains, and can also be thought of as guardians of such places. Most need to be approached carefully, as they can be extremely temperamental. They react well to genuine emotions of sympathy, trust, and the wishing of a witch to learn, and can react quite detrimentally to cynical or disrespectful thoughts, since these creatures react to emotions and feelings, not to the spoken word. This kind of elemental does not, as a rule, move around, but the Old Craft witch should be able to differentiate between the energies of the spirits residing in the cultivated lowlands and those of the rugged uplands

The powerful energies of these locations are especially strong where flowing water is continually reshaping the landscape, and the effects of its erosive power are evident all around. When rainwater falls on mountain slopes and hillsides, it runs downhill, cutting small channels in the rock called rills, which can deepen with further rainfall to form gullies. In these barren uplands we also encounter what geologists called 'karst' scenery that is characteristic of limestone and dolomitic rock landscapes – or 'limestone pavements'. Karst scenery is formed in regions where moderate to heavy rain falls onto surface limestone, or lapié. Water drains into the ground along restricted pathways, through well-defined points, rather than penetrating the rocky surface. A number of small, almost imperceptible trickles of water may have to join up before it is clear that a mountain stream is in the making – travelling along a narrow path over a bottomless gulf in an unexplored country.

Apart from the rush of the mountain stream, the only other wild sound to be heard in the uplands is the defiant call of a buzzard or a golden eagle as it soars high overhead; or the chattering scream of the merlin – and if one of these raptors happens to be our own personal power-animal, then we are in good company. The relationship between man and raptor is of ancient lineage and in fact, there is an old Welsh saying that the social station of a man could be judged by the ownership of his hawk and his hound.

According to the *Concise Encyclopaedia of Heraldry*, eagles have a long ancestry as symbols of divine power and warfare, while hawks trace their lineage as sacred birds to ancient Egypt. Already identified with Deity and borrowing the idea from Asia, the eagle (later double-headed) was adopted as the imperial symbol, linking the ruler with the divine. In the early days of chivalry, hawking was one of the principal pastimes of the nobility and, as a result, both hawks and the accoutrements of hawking were used in the heraldic device. There were also strict guidelines as to who could own such a bird as detailed by Dame Juliana Berners (1388) in her *The Boke of St Albans*, a treatise on hunting and hawking.

Gyrfalcon: A tercel [male] gerfalcon is for a king – described as 'the noblest kind of hawk'.

Falcon gentle [a female goshawk] and a *Tercel gentle* [male peregrine falcon] is for a prince.

Falcon of the Rock: For a duke – a peregrine from remote rocky areas, which would be bigger and stronger than other peregrines; could also refer to the Scottish peregrine.

Falcon peregrine or *pelerine:* For an earl.

Bastard hawk: For a baron – may have been a mistake for buzzard, or for *bustard,* which is French for harrier; possibly meaning a hawk of unknown lineage.

Sacre or *Sacrit:* For a knight – sakers were imported European falcons.

Lanare and *Lanrell:* For a squire – a large southern European falcon (Middle English *laner;* Middle French *lanier*).

Merlyn or *Marlyon:* For a lady.

Hoby: For a young man.

Goshawk: For a yeoman.

Tercel: For a poor man – a male goshawk for a modest landowner.

Sparehawk: For a priest – sparrowhawk – a sacred bird in Teutonic mythology.

Myrkyte or *Musket:* For a holy-water clerk – a sparrowhawk – a crossbow bolt named after the bird.

Kesterel: For a knave or servant.

In early English falconry literature, the word 'falcon' referred to a female falcon only, while the word 'hawk' referred to a female hawk. A male hawk or falcon was referred to as a 'tiercel' (or 'tercel') as it was roughly one third less than the female in size. This is more food for thought when considering the type of power-animal to accompanying us on our quest and these historical guidelines may help in focusing on the possibility of a particular raptor in that role.

Here in the uplands, however, we should not ignore the fact that the largest member of the crow family and ancient power-symbol of witchcraft, the raven, can also be found on the mountainside. Or as Guy Cadogan Rothery observes in *Heraldry*: 'Another equally long-pedigreed feathered messenger from the regions of shadow was the raven, usually styled a 'corbie'.' They have always been held in awe by a wide variety of cultures from around the world.

Our mid-German Arian ancestors venerated the birds, so did the Danes, as certainly did the Celts of the western parts of our land. A raven standard was borne by the Danes who invaded Britain in 787, and fell to Alfred at the battle of Westbury some hundred years later... To this day, the vanished King Arthur circles about our islands and Brittany in the form of a gigantic raven, awaiting the opportune time to reappear as ruler of the United Brittanies. With such a record of warfaring and wisdom, the raven was always much favoured by heralds, and is specially prominent as a crest.

Perhaps we can now understand the importance of identifying with a power-animal that can accompanying us to these dizzy heights – one that can act as our guide and interpreter of the signs and sigils we discover along the way in this hostile environment. Although we have no human companions on our quest, the comfort of having a familiar creature that is looking out for us on both a physical and a mystical level adds to the feeling of companionship.

The Journey Continues...

The saying 'as fresh as a mountain stream' is a well-used cliché, but one that symbolises the simplicity and picturesque imagery of shallow, rippling water flowing over a crystal clear stream-bed and between the enormous rocks on its banks. A mountain stream also has its own distinctive sound of swift-flowing water tripping over smooth, rounded stones; it can also be a thunderous roar when, fuelled by heavy rainfall, it cascades down the mountain side in a column of white water.

For comparison, again we will use an established Shinto analogy that contrasts simplicity with complexity that is mirrored within Nature with the natural state of flux. It reminds us to balance the two principles and integrate them into our lives. According to Aidan Rankin's observations in *Shinto: A Celebration of Life*, here there is no separation between matter and spirit, as there is in world-renouncing spiritual paths or 'scientific' materialism.

From a Shinto perspective, an over-emphasis on the material generates neurosis and discontent. An over-emphasis on the spiritual can lead to an entrenched conservatism and social injustice, or an emphasis on rituals and traditions as ends in themselves, rather than for their inner meanings. As with continuity and change, one cannot work effectively without the other.

The mountain stream also represents a certain single-mindedness as demonstrated by the power of the water that will find the quickest, and most direct route to the sea. As several of these streams merge lower down the mountain, they produce a wider, rocky cascade of sylvan beauty that flows through the tree line to join with the upper reaches of the river. An excellent analogy for the single-mindedness of the witch – symbolically reflected in the merging of the One with the Whole.

Try This Exercise:

Whenever we talk about magical practice, the subject of balance (or equilibrium) will arise, without which, magic cannot work. It has been the norm in recent years to look at this 'balance' in terms of the equality of male/female (i.e. God/Goddess) as a Pair of Opposites and, in many cases in the sole energy of the feminine principle. Whatever the books may say, this is not the true magical meaning of equilibrium.

In Coven of the Scales we use an exercise involving a Pair of Opposites: salt (Earth) and water (Water) with the equilibrated Third – the catalyst – being temperature (Fire – even ice 'burns'). The process even produces evaporation (Air) for an all-round magical exercise! We use tools (a glass container, heating apparatus, a stirring implement) and ritual (the process of setting up the experiment and the application) to create something different and/or wonderful. In this case, the perfect crystal. What happens if we side step the prescribed bounds of the ritual or experiment (i.e. the temperature threshold)? The result is *similar*, but it is an imperfect or deformed crystal. If we just dissolved the salt in the water then 'in the absence of any change in the external conditions [i.e. the addition of equilibrated Third, or catalyst], things will remain this way forever'.

All forms of magic must have this imbalance for the operation to come to fruition, and without a full understanding of its application, our magic will be neutralised, sterile and dysfunctional. Try breaking down your own magical workings into the three components of the Pair of Opposites and identify the catalyst that makes things work.

Chapter Twelve

Keeping Silence (Source)

Mystify: To make mysterious, obscure or secret; to involve in mystery.
[*Chambers Concise Dictionary*]

The terms gateways, portals and doorways speak for themselves, and as a witch's magical ability develops these psychic gateways will begin to open – maybe in one or even several directions simultaneously. Personal advancement along the Old Craft Path depends on an individual's willingness to pass through or stay put, since these gateways open as a result of personal progress serving as an indication that the time has come to move on and to climb to the next level.

Sometimes this transition can be difficult and painful, but in magical learning everything has a reason, so we must never ignore the opportunity, no matter how strange or vague it feels. The price of an Old Craft witch's progress can be exacting, but the end result is well worth it; to ignore it will only result in *personal* loss (in terms of both spiritual and magical development). In time, the same situation will return and the trial begins all over again. If the opportunity is not taken, it may be many years along the line before it occurs again, in which case there are many years lost in an individual's progress as it will be akin to starting anew; or it may not occur again in this lifetime.

Certain gateways or portals can appear in Circle; during meditation; or in a dream, but we should not be afraid of these blinding flashes of inspiration, as they only appear when the 'powers that be' feel that we are ready for them. For an experienced witch it may be a boot in the bustle to suggest they've spent long enough at a particular level and that it's time to take the next step. Not taking the chance on these new openings will be the individual's loss, since those who have chosen *not* to pass through these minor gateways, even after many years of practice, remain at exactly the same level as when they first began. Their magic and understanding has never altered; their progression halted due to their own fear and misunderstanding. They have tried to batter down the doors for years without success; the true Old Craft witch finds that the door swings open at just the lightest touch of a finger when the time is right.

We have now almost reached the end of our journey, but it is probably not what we expected to find, here at the source of all things. Rain and melting snow are the raw material of rivers; some seep through the soil to form underground lakes, or to be soaked up by porous rocks; some is evaporated by the sun ultimately to fall again as rain feeding the tiny watercourses that eventually join together forming swift running mountain streams.

As far as the natural landscape is concerned, a reverence for mountains and a fascination with their sanctity has long been a marked feature of many cultures. In addition, countless other natural features are also held to be sacred – almost every distinct rocky outcrop, river, hill and waterfall is likely to have some important story or legend associated with it. Christopher Tilley, our lecturer in anthropology and archaeology, believes that the Neolithic monuments found in these locations act as a 'camera lens' focussing attention on landscape features such as rock outcrops, river valleys, mountain spurs in their immediate surroundings.

In movement on a path through the landscape something is constantly slipping away and something is constantly gained in a relational tactile world of impressions, signs, sights, smells and physical sensations. To understand the landscape truly it must be felt, but to convey some of this feeling to others it has to be talked about, recounted, or written and depicted. On the process of movement a landscape unfolds or unravels before an observer ... The path may be a symbol not only of interconnectedness and social relations but of movement through life.

While in *Continents in Collision*, Russell Miller observes: 'Mountains, the most spectacular issue of the geological processes that shape the Earth's crust, defied comprehension for centuries.' What were the forces that could have twisted the landscape so dramatically? Eventually scientists evolved the theory of plate tectonics by studying an unfamiliar mountain range – the 40,000-mile-long system of ridges that pattern the floors of the Earth's *ocean* basin – that explained why the presence of fossilised sea creatures could be found in high alpine slopes. The mountains, with all their associated mysteries, began to make sense but, viewed from the perspective of plate tectonic movement, the mountains seem even more awesome than ever!

Despite the rapidly established utility of plate tectonics as a framework for understanding the features of the earth, a great mystery remains. What force, or combination of forces, could possibly provide the energy needed to move these huge slabs of lithosphere over the face of the globe? Studies of gravity, magnetism, heat flow and seismic waves have helped build a rudimentary picture of what may be going on in the interior of the planet, but the difficulties of gaining more detailed understanding are immense.

A researcher is said to have likened these studies to 'trying to figure out the inner workings of a piano by listening to the noise it makes while falling down a flight of stairs', which might well apply to many things of a magical or mystical nature. We are aware of these great natural forces and know that we can draw upon this energy for magical working – but the closer we get to the 'source' the more powerful and dangerous they become. And the more awesome and mysterious.

In other words, the upper slopes of the mountain and the Path leading to it become a metaphor for the Source of all things, seen in the barest trickle of water between immense rocks. Understandably, in returning to the protocols of Shinto, we can draw a parallel with this life religion that is primarily concerned with the here and now, the abundance of Nature, and with many of its ancestral spirits dwelling on a sacred peak in the mountainous regions in the heartland of Japan. On this windswept mountain side, where Neolithic monuments bear testament to the fact that *our* Ancestors indentified with the mystical power of the elements, we are coming to the end of our journey. We accept that the strength of our faith is linked to our culture and experience, as well as personal temperament or choice of Tradition, and that observing Nature is an equally valid expression of spirituality as meditation within the Circle.

What matters is attitude and frame of mind. In the same way, it is ultimately unimportant whether we ultimately focus on an abstract concept of divine power or a specific Deity in whom we invests certain specific qualities. Nor does it much matter how that Deity is conceived since all deities are embodiments of the One.

The Journey Continues...

In *Shinto: A Celebration of Life*, Aidan Rankin explains that with Shinto, the starting point is the intuitive power of the mind and its relationship to the spiritual dimension. We touched briefly on the subject of archetypes in Chapter Three, but these are more than mere creations of the mind; they are representations of something that exists outside, as much as within the human psyche.

The primordial images are therefore images of Kami [God or spirit] power. That power is the animating principle of the universe, uniting (as in dreams) past, present and future, conscious and unconscious, matter and spirit. Shinto practice begins with an acceptance that products of the human imagination that put us in touch with that higher world are in themselves real.

It therefore does not matter whether specific deities 'exist' or not, or whether the myths and legends that surround them are literally true – we behave as if they do. And this is one of the key mysteries of magical knowledge.

These archetypal images are built into our unconscious minds without any help from memory, much like animal instinct. If we reconnect with this inner world, we can re-enter the realm of the archetypes – a realm that is part of the Anima Mundi and part of our own personal Universe. To better understand the symbolism of these archetypal images, we can do no better than study the Major Arcana of the Tarot, since the majority of Old Craft witches have a highly developed working knowledge of this particular branch of divination. The choice of Tarot deck is, of course, a very personal one and must be acquired by intuition rather than recommendation. Familiarise ourselves with the archetypes represented by the Major Arcana and we won't go far wrong in beginning to interpret the esoteric imagery of myth and legend in the cards and recognise exactly what these symbols mean. For example:

0 The Fool
The universal concept of the **Trickster**, who is a subtle blend of innocence and cunning, like the eternal child; a guide or messenger; the joker in the pack; the mythological Green Man, Harlequin, Harpocrates, Dionysus/Bacchus, Hermes, Inari, Loki and Coyote.

I The Magus (or Juggler)

The cross-cultural **Magician** of myth and legend, who is also our mentor and guide, personified by Thoth, Hermes Trismegistus, Haniman, Odin, Merlin or Gandalf.

II Priestess

The **Wise Woman** and the female counterpart of the Hierophant, who instructs in the art of occult knowledge embodied in such deities as Isis, Artemis, Ceres/Demeter, Athena and Neith.

III Empress

The beneficent **Queen** and the epitome of charity and kindness portrayed by deities such as Hera, Aphrodite, Nephthys and Izanami.

IV Emperor

A great **King**, a wise and powerful ruler: all that is positive in the masculine persona, represented by King Arthur and King Solomon; Izanagi, Amun and Herakles.

V Hierophant

The **Teacher** who imparts esoteric knowledge to the people, in a practical and oral way they can understand such as Aesculapius, Imhotep, Okininushi and Cheiron.

VI The Lovers (or The Brothers)

This card represents the alchemical **Union** of opposites on all levels; the balance of opposites or equilibrium as in Yin and Yang; and the mystical unions of Cain and Abel/Osiris and Set.

VII Chariot

A martial symbol of **Victory** in the face of overwhelming odds typified by Mithras, Athena, Neith, Ares/Mars, Hachiman, Thor and Achilles.

VIII Adjustment (or Justice)

The concept of **Justice** being tempered with Mercy; and Mercy tempered with Justice; a state of Equilibrium symbolised by Ma'at, Fudo Myoo, Karma, Nemesis and Varuna.

IX Hermit

The card signifies the silence surrounding **Inner Knowledge** and that which must be sought after, represented by Persephone, Pwyll, Demeter, Geb and Amaterasu.

X Wheel of Fortune

A change of **Fortune** or circumstances – and usually for the better, symbolised by Fortuna and Fukurokuju.

XI Strength (or Lust)

This card symbolises an inner **Strength** that can unexpectedly come to the surface in the most unlikely of persons or situations, and implies far more than 'strength' in the ordinary sense of the word. It is an abstract representation of spiritual life and virility – 'My strength is as the strength of ten, because my heart is pure'.

XII Hanged Man

Redemption through sacrifice and **Submission** to the Divine Will; as in the universal myth of the sacrificial Dying God represented by Geb/Osiris, William Rufus, Adonis, Orpheus, Baldr, Attis.

XIII Death

In esoteric terms, the **Passing** from one stage to another; the universal link between material and spiritual, but always depicted as a skeleton with a scythe or a sword.

Represented by Saturn, the original male creative God and 'that elemental nature of things which is not destroyed by the ordinary changes which occur on the operations of Nature'.

XIV Art (or Temperance)

The symbol of **Personal Control** over an indulgence of the natural appetites and passions; also the alchemical fusing of Fire and Water, as the fertility of the Earth is maintained by rain and sun as represented by the Green Man, Geb, Priapos and Ceres.

XV Devil

The card is often referred to as Pan, or Pan Pangenetor, the All-Begetter, and the force of **Unbridled Nature** represented by the Horned God. The image represents creative energy in its most material form; it is 'divinely unscrupulous, sublimely careless of result'.

XVI Tower

The symbolic destruction of all that is important/prominent ... but not always in a negative form – probably more accurately **Liberation** from the confinement of organised life. The throwing off of chains and anything that binds when the bonds are detrimental to the individual's well-being.

XVII Star

The symbol of timeless **Mystery** and the ever-turning cosmos, depicted by Nut 'our Lady of the Starry Heavens', who holds a golden cup high above her head, from which she pours the ethereal water representing the 'inexhaustible possibilities of existence. Her left hand holds a silver cup from which she pours the immortal liquor of life.'

XVIII Moon

The archetypal suggestion of **Illusion**, often representing standing on the brink of important change; 'This is the threshold of life; this is the threshold of death; All is doubtful, all is mysterious, all is intoxicating'. This is the realm of Thoth, Diana/Artemis, Tsukiyomi and the 'watcher in the twilight' Anubis.

XIX Sun

The ultimate symbol of **Light**, warmth and strength; the Lord of Light, Life, Liberty and Love represented by Amaterasu, Apollo, Atum-Re, Helios and Mithras.

XX Judgement (or The Aeon)

The card represents **Judgement** in its widest possible context – final decision concerning the past and a new current for the future with life progressing a little further along the Path, presided over by Ma'at and Solomon.

XXI Universe (or World)

Representing the macrocosm and the microcosm – All.

NB: The above is not a complete list of correspondences and can be added to as appropriate.

In *Le Symbolisme Hermetique* we are told that these archetypal symbols are designed to arouse a thought by means of suggestion 'and thus cause the truth which lies hidden in our consciousness to reveal itself. A symbol that can be studied from an infinite number of points of view and each thinker has the right to discover in a symbol a new meaning corresponding to the logic of his own conception.'

A Tarot deck usually comes with its own booklet giving details of the traditional interpretation of the cards; ultimately the cards will speak to you – but the messages may not be those given in the popular books. Eventually one will have a stronger 'voice' than the rest and this will become *your* card, regardless of the representation or traditional interpretation. Drawing this card will always have a special significance for you alone, and can be used as a personal gateway for visuali-sation and meditation.

Try This Exercise:

As Chet Raymo also reminds us, no part of our environment is so rich an archive of other intelligences as the night sky. 'The night is a repository of human cultural history. The names of the stars are entries in a family album that shows us what we have been and what we have become.'

And if we don't know our way around these celestial archetypes, here is a good place to start – with the stars associated with the northern sky and the magical 'Place of Power'. Here Draco coils around the North Celestial Pole, guarding the 'still point in the turning world' as the Dweller on the Threshold at the doorway between Time and Eternity. In *The Box of Stars* we discover that around 3000 BC Thuban, the main star in Draco at the centre of the dragon's body, was the Pole Star, which gave the appearance of the whole constellation swinging around this central star. 'It could be seen by both day and night from the bottom of the main, central passage of the Great Pyramid.' Today, the Pole Star is Polaris in the tail of Ursa Minor, the Little Bear.

In the ancient world, star worship was almost universal and we can continue this observance by locating those other two giants of the North Celestial Pole:

- **Ursa Major:** In ancient Greece and Babylon, in India and in North America on early times, Ursa Major, the best-known constellation in the northern sky, has been seen as a she-bear. It is also known as the Big Dipper, the Plough and Charlie's Wain. Its two brightest stars, Mizar and Alcor, were traditionally used as an eyesight test by the military.
- **Cassiopeia:** This constellation is an easily recognisable W-shape and is on view all year round from the northern latitudes; it is not visible from the Southern Hemisphere.

As a witch, we will already be familiar with the 'Place of Power' but by using these stars we can immediately lock on to it in a silent act of homage. Catherine Tennant's *The Box of Stars* is a practical and informative guide to finding our way around the heavens.

Chapter Thirteen

To the Edge of Dream (Cavern)

Mystique: Incommunicable spirit, gift or quality; the secret of an art, known to its inspired practitioners; sense of mystery; remoteness from the ordinary, and power or skill surrounding a person, activity, etc.,
[*Chambers Concise Dictionary*]

Beneath our limestone hills and mountains are series after series of deep caves systems, carved out of the stone by the action of countless years of corroding water. They form our last truly wild places, being remote and difficult of access but, 'What,' asks Robert Gibbons in *The High Kingdom*, 'could be more mysterious than an ancient, rock-bound chasm opening into the Earth's surface, gulping a fast flowing stream into the darkness below?' So here we are ... we're standing on the roof of the world and hopefully our view will be a clear one. From here we can see just how far we've travelled and appreciate just how steep that final climb turned out to be. But we've made it. Our perceptions may have altered – perhaps only slightly – but hopefully we've reached a new understanding about both our inner and outer selves.

In *Underground Worlds*, Donald Dale Jackson opens the 'Lure of the Abyss' with the words:

'My hair stood on end, my teeth chattered, my limbs trembled,' declared one of literature's most famous cavers as he entered a shaft and began the epic adventure recounted in Jules Verne's *Journey to the Centre of the Earth*. Although Verne's tale is entirely fictional, he could not have captured better the misgivings many cavers feel as they step into dark and mysterious subterranean worlds.

Caves have always played an important part in magico-mystical observances; prehistoric man interred his dead in caves, while the Graeco-Roman Mystery traditions used caves for initiatory purposes. Traditional British Old Craft often had a cave as its meeting place rather than an open air gathering as this extract from Bob Clay-Egerton's *Coven of the Scales* reveals:

Since the National (Dis)Trust took over the Cheshire power-zone, archaeological site and beauty spot at Alderley Edge, there have been changes which have affected occultists who have, for many decades, used this ancient and important site … Still open is the CCH Mine, the copper and cobalt mine, which is in reality an exploration level dating from the mid-1800s. It has just outside the entrance the 'Icene Stone' a large bunter sandstone block which was frequently used as an altar. In the past, the CCH Mine was often used for initiation rituals. Though the entrance is quite high, it soon drops to a height of about 6 feet and narrows to a width of around 4 feet. At the end one has to get onto one's hand and knees to enter a small, sandy chamber, roughly oval and about 6 feet wide, 10 feet long and 5 feet high. At each end of the oval is a small silted up passageway which, for ritual purposes, simulates a womb.

Alas, access is also now unavailable to the 'Great Adit'. This flooded passageway runs from the foot of a hillside under the main part of the Edge. Once connecting by shafts, the side entrance to the CCH Mine, the Engine Vein Mine reached as far as the end of a mine in the Artist's Lane Valley. In places, the walls of this passage are green (malachite) and the roof blue (azurite) from the cupriferous arsenical salts. The passage, as late as 1948, was traversed by means of a wooden boat, blunt at each end, no bows at all. In one form of initiation, a pre-initiated was carried down this passage for about three-quarters of a mile to where the passage widened slightly and it was possible to land on a sandy bank.

The pre-initiated was landed on this bank and provided with a quarter inch of candle. The candle was lit and the boat departed, leaving the postulant alone in what was soon to become total darkness. The experience of over 24-hours alone in total darkness, under many feet of solid rock, in utter silence, with even the water not moving, is perhaps the nearest thing one can come to what equates with having passed, with perception, into death and been buried. When, finally the water begins to move, you hear the slight sounds of the approaching boat and at last see, far off, the faint glimmer of light, you have become a new person. You are, in some ways, re-born.

All initiations are, in a sense 'self-initiations', for realisation, awareness comes from within the initiate's subconscious. Ritual and the presence of witnesses, human and/ or spiritual is only necessary to assist in conditioning the mind to an acceptance of a new state of being. Of all rituals, those which more closely symbolise the death of the former personality, and the birth of a new one, are perhaps the most effective. Of such rituals, the actual immurement for a period underground, may well be the most effective and longest lasting.

These are the thoughts that go through our mind as we stand at the entrance to the cavern, in what is known as the 'twilight zone', which is the limit of light penetration from the outside. There is a trickle of sharp, clear water edged by moss by our feet which encourages us to penetrate deeper into the darkness. The dark 'transition zone' beyond has a variable climate but we notice that the air temperature is a few degrees warmer. By the rim of the pool, rimstone creates a natural cascade where the water from the inner pool slowly overflows, while above our heads, straw stalactites are in the process of being formed.

In the darkness at the rear of the inner cavern the temperature is warm and humid; the walls are lined with flowstone, where a film of water flows down a sloping surface, leaving a deposit of smooth calcite. The rock walls are limestone and the floor is of sticky orange-brown clay; the only other colours thrown up by our artificial light are the varied hues of brown, interrupted by the glistening white of extraordinary stalactite and stalagmite formations built up over the course of many years from minerals in the constantly dripping water into fantastic architectural shapes and patterns. This is a natural grotto with stalactites hanging from the ceiling and in its centre, a natural pool of still, dark water.

> Water, the shaper of caves, is a versatile as well as patient worker; even as it completes the excavation of a gigantic chamber in the earth, it is attending to the infinitely delicate task of decoration. Setting microscopic crystals of mineral one upon another, the slowly moving liquid crafts an eerie gallery of sculpture whose variety and beauty can be breathtaking.
> *Underground Worlds*, Donald Dale Jackson

This confining atmosphere also plays an important part in the ascetic disciplines of Shinto, and is called *komori*, meaning seclusion, preferably in the darkness of a cave. Like its association with the waterfall, the power-giving qualities of seclusion in darkness gestate and grow, 'until it bursts its covering and emerges into the world'. And here we reminder ourselves of Chet Raymo's words that darkness is the mother of beauty, that extinction of light is a revelation ... And he is right in his observation that few people willingly choose to walk the dark path, 'to enter the dark wood, to feel the knot of fear in the stomach, or to live in the black cave of the sleepless night. But then, unexpectedly the truth emerges. The light of the mind returns bearing extraordinary gifts.'

It is also ironic that at the higher levels of esoteric philosophy [*The Hollow Tree*] the Temple of Binah is depicted as having been hewn from bare, living rock in order to give the impression of Timelessness, since it reaches back in time to when the Earth was in a state of upheaval. Binah represents the female potency of the Universe; the sacred image of the 'Terrible Mother' that we discussed in an earlier chapter.

The floor is hard-packed earth and the altar is a large boulder with a natural hollow at the top which holds the sacred flame. There are four doors flanked by pillars of stone and the air is perfumed with myrrh...

The Temple of Chokmah, however, represents the male potency of the Universe; the 'Great Stimulator' and appears as a huge stone-henge monument constructed of granite.

The floor is polished granite and so is the altar, on top of which burns a simple wood fire – the first flame. There are four doors flanked by granite columns and the air is perfumed with musk.

Each of the Pair of Opposites throws light on the other and is incomprehensible alone. In Chokmah and Binah we have the archetypal Positive and Negative; the primordial Maleness and Femaleness and from this Pair of Opposites the Pillars of the Universe spring. By contrast, the Temple of Malkuth (the Sphere of Earth) from where we take the decision to make the first irreversible step on the Path, the Temple is much more impressive:

The floor is made up of black and white squares; in the centre is the altar constructed from a double cube (one on top of the other) and covered by a white cloth. On the altar is a deep blue crystal bowl in which burns the sacred flame. Overhead is the bronze lamp for the burning of incense and the Temple is filled with the perfume of Dittany of Crete. At the four quarters a light burns for each of the four elements. On the eastern wall there are two pillars flanking three doors – a black one to the left and a silver one to the right.

The significance of the reversal of 'wealth' in this lower realm is mere illusion in order to mislead, and as Dion Fortune points out in *The Mystical Qabalah*: 'We are dealing with cosmic principles, not personalities; and even the symbols under which they are presented gives us insight if we have eyes to see.'

The Journey Continues...

And one thing that we have probably discovered on our journey is that God *is* out there. This may not be the divine presence of the religious textbooks but Marcus Chown, writing in *The Magic Furnace*, produces a more than reasonable argument for the existence of God from the *scientist's* point of view. In this extraordinary account of how modern science unravelled the mystery of atoms, we also learn that our individual bodies contain atoms 'forged in the blistering furnaces deep inside stars and blasted into space by stellar explosions that blazed brighter than a billion suns'.

Is this far-fetched science-fiction? Not at all, for according to scientific data the iron in our blood, the calcium in our bones and the oxygen in our lungs contain atoms blown across unimaginable gulfs of space and time. Going back to ancient times, astrologers claimed that people's lives were ruled by the stars and as *The Magic Furnace* explains, they were right in essence if not in detail. Twentieth century science has discovered that we are far more intimately connected to events in the cosmos that anyone ever dared imagine, simply because those atoms that we carry around in our bodies originated in deep space.

These atoms were thrown out into space by the collapse of a giant star, adding to the swirling mass of gas and dust from which new stars were created. Eventually a cloud of gas and dust formed on the edge of the Milky Way, and in the cooling process the heavy elements in the cloud became incorporated into a new sun and its family of planets. In turn these elements became part of the Earth and ultimately the first primitive living cells ... which means that 'every one of us was quite literally made in heaven. Each and every one of us is stardust made flesh.'

So scientific discovery compounds the mystical realisation of eternity and the state of 'deathlessness within oneself from which the whole Universe of change and time and space is excluded'. If we comprise atoms that have been part of the cosmic ballet for close on five-billion years then the case for 'God' is surely proven. We are no longer seeking amongst the doctrine and dogma of Earth-bound faith, but in the vast energy fields that exist in time and space.

Try This Exercise:

The pilgrim who would find his way to the edge of the galaxies and to the beginning of time must forgo daylight's easy colour and launch himself on the black-and-white sea of the night and in those huge spaces find stars the colours of damson, crocus, grape and straw. The quest will perhaps require more courage than you or I can bear...
Chet Raymo, *The Soul of the Night*.

Over time, we *must* become familiar with the stars – and not with an astrologer's eye – but from an astronomer's perspective. This exercise should be performed outdoors on a clear night before or just after the dark of the moon. Your eyes will need 20 minutes to adjust to night vision so use the time to make yourself comfortable. Ensure that you are wearing something warm if you are doing this in winter. As you will need to spend some time with your head tilted back, it is a good idea to spend this waiting time arranging cushions or setting a reclining chair so that you can gaze at the heavens in comfort.

After 20 minutes, look up into the sky again, and you will be surprised how many more stars you can see now that your eyes have made the adjustment. Watch Cassiopeia and Ursa Major in their slow heavenly dance and think about the energies of male and female weaving their magical dance across the night skies. Let your eyes be drawn towards the brightest star that you can see and concentrate all your effort into reaching out to this star with your mind. Let the charm *'listen and glisten'* run repetitively through your mind over and over again the whole time ...

See what happens ... make notes on your return.

The Journey Ends ... Twilight Zone

The paper-trail ends here in the twilight zone – because, to be honest, that's all we've been following. Despite the fact that we have been seriously following the Path to the Mysteries, we discover there is no book printed that *can* offer a comprehensive guide to the subject. As we were warned at the beginning, that like smoke from the Abyss, curling tendrils of esoteric jargon cloud the issue until we choke on the obscuring fumes of our own research. Infernal shadows of illusion still hound and harry the unwary along a series of concealing alleyways with conflicting signposts and deliberately obtuse instructions. We follow the rock-strewn pathway, through those endless sloping corridors to a distorted hall of mirrors, where we emerge into the light no wiser than when we first began our quest. We have reached the limit of light penetration into this twilight zone – we cannot go further and must also recall Alan Richardson's world-weary words at the beginning:

> In magic there are the Lesser and Greater Mysteries. The former are the basic teachings whose intellectual content are available to all. The Greater Mysteries can only be understood through experience; they cannot be taught in words. The best that can be done is to provide symbols that the student may use as lenses to bring into focus his own blurred intimations of something greater in this world than himself. That is why it is useless searching books for any True Secret. It does not exist. Books and teachers can only give a few inadequate methods to reach the wisdom that is nowhere else but within the seeker.

With the benefit of hindsight, however, it may often appear as though we *have* followed a straight line towards our destiny. That we have moved from person to person, from discovery to discovery, from revelation to revelation but we are still nowhere near our goal. What we will have come to understand is that the Mysteries are not there for the asking; that entry has to be earned over a span of many years. All *Traditional Witchcraft and the Path to the Mysteries* can do is prepare the seeker for the arduous trials that lie ahead and warn that the pathway is littered with the astral bodies of those who have given up the quest. Perhaps the ultimate revelation is that which has been described as 'the flight of the alone to the Alone'; the realisation that we can be led to the Gateway but we must pass through alone; that there is no one to help us beyond the Gateway once we have passed beyond the threshold of human experience.

When we finally learn how to use our astral senses there should no longer be any confusion, because although Otherworld mirrors certain correspondences with the material one, there is a perfect distinction between the two. Once recognised, these correspondences sing out loud and clear as to their place in the scheme of things and act as signposts on either side of the Gateway. These signposts can be found in the most unlikely places and by using references and examples from other beliefs and cultures, we can often see that 'truth' more clearly. This 'truth', however, will often be viewed as elitist because as Daniel A Schulke observed: *'All of these traditions share a common feature of extreme selectivity when it comes to prospective members, and the willingness to reject those proven unfit for the work.'*

We should also be aware of what might be described as 'opportunities' – situations that offer a *kensho* experiences that we may fail to recognise, or ignore because they do not seem important enough. Once we have embarked upon the quest *everything* becomes part of the spiritual/mystical ordeal. The main test at this point is the realisation that any incident may have a spiritual significance and if we fail to grasp its importance, to understand that if we do not pursue the opportunity, the way could be shut forever. By failing to appreciate the opportunity at its full value we may miss the supreme chance of a lifetime since the way could be the Gateway to Otherworld that we seek.

Unfortunately there will always be those who believe that Initiation into the Mysteries will confer power and riches, and it is as well to return to the first chapter and reflect on what it is that is the cornerstone of a witch's faith and ask again those three basic questions:

What does a witch hold to be the three basic beliefs?

1. That there is one originating 'force'
2. That this force is completely natural
3. That this natural force can be used by mankind

What does a witch ask for?

1. Sufficient nourishment (food and/or knowledge)
2. Shelter from the elements (also with a hidden meaning)
3. Love (again with hidden meaning)

What does a witch seek?

1. Knowledge, plus wisdom, plus understanding
2. Belief in tolerance and balance
3. The rule of natural law

These simple tenets of faith need to be enshrined in our memory because they allow us to perceive the simplicity at the heart of creation. That indefinable 'something' which is impossible to grasp without the help of divinity, for it is beyond language, and yet it is so simple that we know that it is a part of us just as we are part of that which is enacted, that which is shown, and that which is spoken. We see the world as it is now and the Otherworld that is to come; the life we live now and the cosmic spiral of life that allows us to glimpse eternity. In simple terms: the Initiated do not learn anything so much as feel certain emotions and are put into a certain frame of mind.

Nevertheless, we do develop a new way of looking at the world, as Aleister Crowley observes in *Confessions*:

> In rock climbing and travelling through mountain forests one sees nature in perfection. At every turn, the foreground picks out special spots of the background for attention, so that there is a constant succession of varying pictures. The eye is no longer bewildered by being asked to take in too much at once; and the effect of the distance is immensely heightened by contrasts with the foreground.

There is an echo here of the lessons learned from Shinto when observing Nature, in that a distant mountain can be awesome, but a strategically placed branch in the foreground makes it spectacular, or the difference between a souvenir snapshot and an art photograph. Our witch's eye is drawn to the beauty.

Again we return to that observation that Old Craft learning is about 40 percent information and 60 percent intuition, and realising when intuition is telling us that we don't have all the information. And it should be obvious that although we have received all this information about what to expect during our quest, it will be a long road ahead before we even reach that mystical 'gate of conversion' – that spiritual point of no return that enables us to see what a short way we've travelled and not fool ourselves into believing that we have arrived.

We have already completed the journey from the seashore to the mountain in our mind and are alert to the dangers we will encounter along the way. We have been warned that this will entail stepping from a well-worn Path into a fog that conceals metaphorical quick sands, sheer rock and inhospitable wilderness; hopefully we can walk on and observe that which was previously hidden, and although we may have received guidance and encouragement from a teacher, *we must walk on alone.*

There are times, however, when the way is barred to us for no apparent reason. As Crowley is his wisdom also observed:

Physical ability and moral determination count for nothing. It is impossible to perform the simplest act when the Gods say 'No'. I have no idea how they bring pressure to bear on such occasions; I only know that it is irresistible. One may be wholeheartedly eager to do something which is as easy as falling off a log; and yet it is impossible.

This sensation we will encounter time and time again on a mystical quest on both the physical and astral planes, when an invisible barrier prevents us from going further. 'The reason is that no sooner does a man make up his mind to enter the Path of the Wise than he rouses automatically the supreme hostility of every force, internal or external, in his sphere.' We push against the barrier and rail against the unfairness but the way remains shut; perhaps our Guardian has thrown up a protective shield for some reason best know to itself – but in time the barrier dissolves for no apparent reason and we are free to go on our way.

The source for the material contained in *Traditional Witchcraft and the Path to the Mysteries* is based on the teachings from a British-based Old Craft coven led by Aleister (Bob) and Mériém Clay-Egerton that could trace its roots in Cheshire, England, back to the 1800s. Their view was that it is not unreasonable to surmise that Old Craft probably retains features of the native shamanic practices of the ancient Briton, since the term 'shamanism' describes the supernatural powers practitioners channel from the spirit world for healing, divination and the conducting of souls – all of which are the natural province of an Old Craft practitioner where it is viewed as 'an isolated or peripheral phenomenon', rather than the overt devotional practices often found in contemporary paganism. As intermediaries between the world of the Ancestors and the living, the Old Craft practitioner maintains direct contact with spirits, whether of Otherworld, 'of plants, animals and other features of the environment, such as the 'master-spirits' (e.g. of rivers or mountains)'.

The *genii loci* or guardians of these locations are some of the strangest spirit beings we encounter since few are able to move from their native area, either because they are 'part of the landscape' or because they are bound to it for some other reason. Although extremely powerful and appearing to possess rational thought, they are 'simply vast, semi-sentient well-springs of magical energy' with the power rarely extending beyond the boundaries of the particular *genii loci*. If a witch is in that location at the time of posing a magical question, the energy may manifest in the form of a divinatory response, simply because a magical practitioner provides a natural conduit for this type of energy.

Christopher Tilley describes this phenomenon in *A Phenomenology of Landscape* as occurring because the landscape has ancestral importance due to it being such an integral part of human development that it abounds with cultural meaning and symbolism. 'Precisely because locales and their landscapes are drawn on in the day-to-day lives and encounters of individuals they possess powers. The spirit of place may be held to reside in a landscape.' Despite different locations giving a variety of explanations for the existence of this 'spirit energy', in a large number of instances the intelligent, magical entity simply develops from the colloquially named 'spirit of place' over a great deal of time. Although this spirit-energy is usually considered to be an 'essence of Deity' rather than the Deity itself, the Old Craft practitioner treats them with the utmost reverence and respect.

Nevertheless, Bob Clay-Egerton brought everything full circle when he described the Power of the One in pure animistic terms:

> The Almighty is everything, physical and non-physical, literally everything and therefore incomprehensible to our finite understanding. Being everything, the Almighty is male *and* female *and* neuter – not just a male entity. All things are created in the image of the Almighty because the Almighty is every part of everything. The Almighty has no specific regard or concern for one species – i.e. mankind, among millions of species on one insignificant minor planet, in an outer arm of a spiral galaxy which is one among millions.

Much of this may be seen as playing with semantics, but in truth, the God forms themselves have changed greatly down through the millennia. It is only by studying myths, legends and folklore, and pulling all the strands together that we can appreciate just how much these have altered. To a pre-dynastic Egyptian, for example, the Goddess Isis was a modest deity identified with Osiris; later her cult spread into Greek and Roman society, becoming so popular in later days that she absorbed the qualities of many of the other deities – male *and* female. Early Christianity found it easier to incorporate the Mother and Child image into its own canon rather than suppress it; while in modern times she has become the greatly diluted Mother Goddess of the international Fellowship of Isis organisation – so far removed from the God-power of the ancient Nile valley that she would be seen as an alien entity by those early worshippers.

The spirits of the landscape, however, have remained constant; they have not altered their form and have only grown more powerful with age. These well-springs of magical energy have not been contaminated because few have known of their existence – apart from the native shamanic practitioners [witches] who have kept the secret down through the ages. In more secluded spots, the spirit-energy of the ancient Britons survives in remote ancient monuments, isolated lakes, the rural landscape, and in the depths of the surviving wildwood with which our hunter-gatherer Ancestors would have been familiar. When the native shamanic practices went into the shadows, these powerful energy spots were deemed unholy and feared by the locals – and as such passed into folklore as those things that are 'never fully remembered and yet never fully forgotten'.

Nevertheless, mystical development is something that happens to an individual when the scales begin to fall from the seeker's eyes, and the world is perceived in a different light. No matter how we decide to express this pursuit of the inconceivable, we have to accept responsibility for our own actions and the repercussions. For the witch who finds these ideas unpalatable, it is best that they don't attempt the journey in the first place, because as we have already discussed, although it is possible to retrace our steps back to safety, the damage is already done. The 'innocence' of thought that kept us happily immersed in coven ritual and relationships will have already evaporated; we will have already come too far to regain that blissful state of ignorance.

Hopefully the true seeker will not be daunted by the trials and tribulations, but as that biblical text says: *'Many are called but few are chosen'*, and this is why those who have completed the journey are referred to in esoteric terms as 'elect'. Neither should it be considered failure if the decision is made not to undertake the journey; or having failed to complete it – since there is no criticism levelled at those who make an informed choice of not forging on ahead that had been based on sound, rational thinking.

So ... all we are left with at the end of our paper-trail that serves as evidence of our intention, is our backpack which feels curiously light after all the years of accumulating the material trappings of the witch. In a front pocket is our pendulum that we use for divination and checking out the landscape; we'll probably have slipped in our favourite deck of Tarot cards 'just in case'. The significance of the witch's knife and cord is more apparent to us now and we know that everything of spiritual importance is contained within these two simple items. We may decide to include an amulet representing our power-animal, which gives us an excuse to include our magical pouch that we've had since the beginning of our studies. Lastly we have the copies of *The Soul of the Night* and *Honey from Stone,* which teach us that we can find words of wisdom in the most unlikely and unexpected of sources.

The bag is packed ... we're ready to go. Time is short, and we have far to travel.

There is always as much difficulty in finding the right closing lines to a book as there is in creating the opening. In this instance we will give the Epilogue over to astrophysicist Chet Raymo, who has so often been our spiritual guide during this journey ...

There is a tendency for us to flee from the wild silence and the wild dark, to pack up our Gods and hunker down behind city walls, to turn the Gods into idols, to kowtow before them and approach their precincts only in the official robes of office. And when we are in the temples, then who will hear the voice crying in the wilderness? Who will hear the reed shaken by the wind? Who will watch the Galaxy rise above the eastern hedge and see a river infinitely deep and crystal clear, a river flowing from the spring that is Creation to the ocean that is Time?

So mote it be.

Sources and Bibliography

Adam's Curse, Bryan Sykes (Corgi)

Atmosphere, Oliver E Allan (Time Life)

The Box of Stars, Catherine Tennant (Bulfinch)

Britain BC, Francis Pryor (HarperCollins)

The Catalpa Bow, Carmen Blacker (Japan Library)

Concise Encyclopaedia of Heraldry, Guy Cadogan Rothery (Bracken)

Continents in Collision, Russell Miller (Time Life)

Coursing and Falconry, Hon. Gerald Lascelles (The Badminton Library)

Earth, ed. Peter Frances (DK)

Edge of the Sea, Russell Sackett (Time Life)

The Essential Difference, Simon Baron-Cohen (Penguin)

Eastern Religions, Ed Michael D Coogan (DPB)

Exploring Spirituality, Suzanne Ruthven and Aeron Medbh-Mara (How To)

Facing the Ocean, Barry Cunliffe (OUP)

The Golden Bough, Sir James Frazer (McMillan)

The Great Religions By Which Men Live, Floyd H Ross and Tynette Hills (Crest)

Honey From Stone, Chet Raymo (Brandon)

The Hollow Tree, Mélusine Draco (ignotus)

The Lore of the Forest, Alexander Porteous (Senate)

Magic Crystals, Sacred Stones, Mélusine Draco (Axis Mundi)

The Mysteries of Mithra, Franz Cumont (Dover)

The Mystical Qabalah, Dion Fortune (Aquarian)

The New Believers, David V. Barrett (Cassell)

The Religion of Ancient Rome, Cyril Bailey (OUP)

The Restless Oceans, A C Whipple (Time Life Books)

Rites and Symbols of Initiation, Mircea Eliade (Harper)

Rivers and Lakes, Laurence Pringle (Time Life)

Seas and Islands, ed Keith Hiscock (Readers Digest)

Secrets of the Seashore, ed Derek Hall (Readers Digest)

Shinto: A Celebration of Life, Aidan Rankin (Mantra)

Traditional Witchcraft for Fields and Hedgerows, Mélusine Draco (Moon Books)

Traditional Witchcraft and the Pagan Revival, Mélusine Draco (Moon Books)

Traditional Witchcraft for the Seashore, Mélusine Draco (Moon Books)

Traditional Witchcraft for Urban Living, Mélusine Draco (Moon Books)

Traditional Witchcraft for Woods and Forests, Mélusine Draco (Moon Books)

The Soul of the Night, Chet Raymo (Prentice-Hall)

Underground Worlds, Donald Dale Jackson (Time Life)

What You Call Time, Suzanne Ruthven (ignotus)

The Winged Bull, Dion Fortune (Aquarian)

The World of Still Water, Robert Gibbons (Readers Digest)

About the Author

Mélusine Draco originally trained in the magical arts of traditional British Old Craft with Bob and Mériém Clay-Egerton. She has been a magical and spiritual instructor for over 20 years, and author of numerous popular books on witchcraft and magic. Her highly individualistic teaching methods and writing draw on ancient sources, supported by academic texts and current archaeological findings. www.covenofthescales.com

Her Traditional Witchcraft series is published by Moon Books (an imprint of John Hunt Publishing): *Traditional Witchcraft for Urban Living, Traditional Witchcraft for the Seashore, Traditional Witchcraft for Fields and Hedgerows* and *Traditional Witchcraft for Woods and Forests* as well as *Traditional Witchcraft and the Pagan Revival* together with *The Dictionary of Mystery and Magic, Magic Crystals, Sacred Stones* (Axis Mundi), *By Spellbook and Candle, Aubry's Dog, Black Horse, White Horse* and *The Atum-Re Revival* (Axis Mundi). All titles are available via the publisher's US distributors or from the different imprints at www.johnhuntpublishing.com.

MOON

BOOKS

Moon Books invites you to begin or deepen your encounter with
Paganism, in all its rich, creative, flourishing forms.